FAITH AND DOCTRINE

FAITH AND DOCTRINE

A Contemporary View

by

Gregory Baum

NEWMAN PRESS

Paramus, N. J.   **New York, N. Y.**

Amsterdam   **Toronto**   **London**

THE DAVID S. SCHAFF LECTURES

In 1965 an annual lectureship was established at Pittsburgh Theological Seminary in honor of the Rev. David S. Schaff (D.D., Illinois; Th.D., Geneva and Prague). Funds for endowing the lectureship were contributed by Dr. Schaff's daughter, Miss Mary L. Schaff, of Washington, D.C., his daughter-in-law, Mrs. Philip H. Schaff, of Youngstown, Ohio, and Miss Margaret Campbell, of Sewickley, Pennsylvania. The lecturers, selected by the faculty of the seminary, may lecture on any subject related to the general field of theological study. The terms of the lectureship stipulate that the lectures are to be published.

The fourth series of lectures on the Schaff foundation, delivered by Father Gregory Baum, of St. Michael's College, University of Toronto, Canada, on October 21-23, 1968, is presented in this volume in expanded and slightly modified form.

Donald G. Miller
President, Pittsburgh Theological Seminary
Pittsburgh, Pennsylvania

NIHIL OBSTAT:
Very Rev. Msgr. William F. Hogan
Censor Librorum

IMPRIMATUR:
✠ Joseph A. Costello
Vicar General, Archdiocese of Newark

February 3, 1969

The Nihil Obstat and Imprimatur are official declarations that a book or pamphlet is free of doctrinal or moral error. No implication is contained therein that those who have granted the Nihil Obstat and Imprimatur agree with the contents, opinions or statements expressed.

Library of Congress
Catalog Card Number: 72-76957

Published by Newman Press
Editorial Office: 304 W. 58th St., N. Y., N. Y. 10019
Business Office: Paramus, New Jersey 07652

Printed and bound in the
United States of America

Contents

v

To
ROBERT MADDEN

Introduction

Changes are taking place in the Catholic Church because Catholics have begun to experience the Gospel in a new way. They may not know exactly what happens to them; they may not be able to put this experience into words and analyze its meaning, but they are quite certain that to be a Christian means something different to them today than it did some years ago. This is true at least for a vast number of Catholics. Recalling the spiritual books and devotions they enjoyed in the past, they realize by comparison how much has changed in their lives. Priests and nuns who have been trained in a definite spirituality are very much aware of this. As they remember the spirituality acquired in novitiate or seminary and the spiritual literature they read at that time, they recognize that the Gospel of Christ has a new meaning for them today. Some Catholics are so far from where they were a few years ago that they find it hard to imagine how they were able to assimilate the inherited religion at one time.

Every authentic development in the Church takes place, first of all, in the hearts of men who seek fidelity to Jesus Christ. Authentic development is the work of the Spirit in the minds of men. Neither theology nor the institution offers the first stimulus. What happens, rather, is that Christians living in a new cultural setting experience the call and the meaning of Christ in a new way. This Spirit-created experience enables theologians to reflect on the Word of God in a new perspective and encourages the ecclesiastical government to promote institutional reforms in the Church.

1

How can we describe this new self-understanding of the Catholic? I wish to describe the new experience of the Gospel by presenting two of its characteristics.

Universal Brotherhood

The first one is the new experience of *universal brotherhood*. Catholics today have a new sense of solidarity and feelings of friendship toward other Christians and toward people belonging to another, or to no religion. When involved with others in the same important issues or sharing with others what is most precious to us, we experience a sense of community that was not open to us before. Today Catholics sometimes experience this sense of community more in mixed gatherings concerned with the crucial issues of human life and society, than they do in the midst of their parish or in conversation with their own bishop.

In the past we were also taught to love other people. But we felt most at home in a Catholic environment. We were a little cautious in regard to others. We thought that our essentially Catholic experience of Christ constituted a barrier which prevented us from sharing the precious things of life with other people. Today this has changed. A new sense of universal brotherhood has developed. What counts for us is not so much whether another person belongs to a specific Church or to any Church at all; what counts is his concern about the important issues in life, about love and the transformation of society, about personal growth and expanding responsibility.

The dogmatic basis for this new experience of universal brotherhood was laid at Vatican II. The conciliar documents teach that the communion created by the Spirit in the Church extends beyond the Church to include not only other Christians

but all men who are open to the Spirit.[1] God is redemptively
present to the whole of humanity, summoning men to growth
and reconciliation. We no longer suppose that Catholics are
bound to one another by a "supernatural" brotherhood and to
other people simply by a "natural" brotherhood, based on
the common human nature created by God. Today the Church
teaches that the brotherhood of man is not natural but redemptive. It is based on the redemptive presence of God to human
life, as revealed to us by Christ and his victory in death and
resurrection.

New Openness to Truth

A second characteristic of the new self-understanding of
Catholics is a new *openness* to truth. Catholics look back over
their lives and marvel at the many things they have learned.
They expect this process to continue in the future. Truth
comes to us from all directions. We are ready to learn from
the most unexpected sources. Whenever we meet a group of
people, enter into a conversation, read a book or see a film,
we expect to learn something. We expect to grow a little by
the truth that is being uttered. This does not mean that Catholics today uncritically swallow everything they hear. No; to
be open to the truth means to be critical. What happens is
that Catholics listen to what is being said to them and ask:
Does it fit? Does it tie in with our christian convictions?
Does it make sense in the light of our faith about life and
God's presence to it? Does it promote growth or regression?
Does it foster friendship or set up obstacles to communication?
If what we hear ties in with our deep convictions about Jesus,

[1] For an analysis of the conciliar texts see G. Baum, "The Self-
Understanding of the Roman Catholic Church at Vatican II", *The
Church and the Churches* (ed. G. Johnston), Toronto, 1967, pp.
86-107.

we are willing to learn. We are even willing to change our minds. Catholics have come to learn that the deep convictions about life and God's presence to it, are strengthened as we change our minds about all kinds of things.

In the past our love of truth took on a different form. We believed that the full truth of Christ, available in the Catholic Church alone, was the great treasure that we had received, and we thought that it was our task to protect this treasure against human thought and values that constituted the culture to which we belonged. While we were willing to learn in many subjects, there were always some subjects in which we thought we had nothing to learn. On the basis of the doctrinal system we had inherited, we made up our minds very quickly as to what we might accept from others. We entered into conversation, we read books and saw films, not to *learn* from others but to *evaluate* the ideals of others in the light of Catholic doctrine. Today Catholics desire to be just as faithful to God's Word made known in Christ and preached by the Church, but they think that this implies openness to truth as it comes to us through historical experience. The truth of the Gospel can be preserved in us only as we remain listeners.

Again, the dogmatic foundation for this new experience of truth was laid, at least implicitly, at Vatican II. For while in the past we tended to regard divine revelation as the teaching of Christ and the apostles, and hence as something finished, Vatican II understood divine revelation as the self-communication of God in his Word which happened from the beginning of human history, which took place in radical fashion in the person of Jesus Christ, and which continues to take place in history through the proclamation of Jesus Christ and, in a less explicit manner, through the experience of human life.[2]

---

[2] See G. Baum, "Vatican II's Constitution on Revelation: History and Interpretation", *Theological Studies,* 28 (1967) 51-75.

Divine revelation is an on-going reality in history. It is completed in Jesus Christ. In him God has revealed himself unconditionally and definitively. But the identical self-communication of God that took place in Jesus Christ continues to take place in the Church. God perpetually reiterates his Word spoken once and for all in Jesus Christ. For this reason fidelity to Christ and his message means a constant readiness to listen, to be open to the truth uttered today, to be ready to learn and, if need be, to be converted again and again.

The Church's Institutional Life

We have described the new Catholic self-awareness by presenting two characteristics: a new sense of universal brotherhood and a new openness to truth. This new experience of the Gospel creates tensions in the institutions. The ecclesiastical institution we have inherited reflects a *past* experience of the Gospel. It was meant to serve the common good of the community as it was then understood. Today, because of the development that has taken place the institution no longer fully embodies what Jesus Christ means to the Catholic community.

Let me make this assertion more explicit. The present ecclesiastical institution does not embody the new sense of brotherhood or the new openness to truth. For instance, the legislation in regard to mixed marriages and the sharing of sacramental communion is based on a Catholic experience and on doctrinal positions that are characteristic of the past. If the Church is open-ended, if the Spirit-created communion in the Catholic Church extends beyond her boundaries to include other Christians and even the unbaptized open to the Spirit, then the issues of mixed marriage and of intercommunion—not to speak of separate schools—appear altogether in a new light.

Today official Catholic teaching has acknowledged that to become more truly herself the Church is in need of other people, of the whole human race; yet, this is not acknowledged in the Church's institutional life.

Neither is the new openness to truth acknowledged in the ecclesiastical institutions. This openness has revealed the central role of dialogue or conversation in the discernment of what we should think and what we should do in the various situations of life. The marvelous experience of Christians today is that in meetings held to solve the problems of the community, they engage in open conversation, listen to one another and, at the end of the process, come to insights and find a course of action, which were not in the minds of any of the participants prior to the conversation. The Spirit present in dialogue creates new understanding. More than that, conversations in which we learn from one another transform us as persons. The very process of dialogue creates in us a new approach to our human environment, which in turn leads to a new self-understanding. Dialogue makes us open to truth in a new way.

The ecclesiastical institution on the whole has not yet acknowledged the process of conversation. Dialogue happened at Vatican II and in some subsequent ecclesiastical gatherings, but on the whole the hierarchy shows few signs that it is seriously interested in the new approach. The ecclesiastical government often determines beforehand how far any conversation can go, what may and may not be called into question, and in which directions the answers are to be found. Sometimes the hierarchy seems to decide policy in advance and uses dialogue with clergy and people as a technique to keep people happy.

The tension in the Church at this time, then, is due to the

new experience of the Gospel in the Catholic community which is at odds with the institutional patterns of the past. What is needed is an institutional reform that embodies the new Catholic self-understanding and the doctrinal reflection on it that the Spirit has produced in the Church.

Doctrinal Development

The new Spirit-created experience of the Gospel, tested by the scriptures and critical theological reflection, has profoundly influenced the conciliar teaching of Vatican II. In my book *The Credibility of the Church Today*,[3] I have tried to show that a startling doctrinal development has taken place at Vatican II. I have analyzed this development as a shift of focus in the proclamation of the Gospel. The central thrust and message of the Gospel today is the Good News about human life, i.e., the Good News not only about what happens to Christians but about what happens to people everywhere. The marvelous reality that God has made known in Jesus Christ is that he is redemptively involved in the lives of all men. The mystery of humanization which the Church proclaims in Christ and the sending of the Spirit, is present not only in the Church where the gifts of Christ are celebrated but also in the rest of mankind where the Word and the gift of God are available to men in a hidden way through the experience of their lives and of history.

This shift of focus in the proclamation of the Gospel demands the re-interpretation of the entire teaching of the Church in the light of the new focus. In *The Credibility of the Church Today* I have tried to interpret Catholic ecclesiology in the light of the new focus. The doctrine of the Church not

[3] G. Baum, *The Credibility of the Church Today* (Herder and Herder, 1968).

only deals with what God is doing in the christian community but makes known, also and especially, how every community of men is threatened by the sin that pervades life and how it is summoned to newness of life by God's self-communication to his people.

In the lectures collected in this book I try to work out the implications of the new focus for the theology of faith. What is faith? What do we mean by the unchanging nature of the christian faith? I wish to show that Catholic theology today can demand a re-interpretation of the Church's entire teaching and at the same time insist on the unchanging nature of the Gospel in which we believe. The new focus also makes christian apologetics appear in a new light. While many Catholic theologians have lost interest in the apologetical problem, I feel that christian theology can never dispense itself from investigating the rational foundation of the believer's option. What are the human reasons for believing? In these lectures I try to develop a new approach to apologetics.

Ultimately the re-interpretation of doctrine in the light of the new focus will have to be applied to the doctrine of God. Is it possible to speak about God and his transcendence in a manner that is in harmony with the contemporary experience of reality? In another study I hope to show that the re-focusing of the Gospel that took place at Vatican II enables us to re-think the problem of God and to speak of God and the entire content of his revelation in terms taken from the significant conflicts of contempory life and in a language that is proper to our day.

I
Faith and Doctrine

We live in a changing world. To our surprise we find that we also live in a changing Church. Much has been happening in the Catholic Church over the last few years. The convocation of Vatican II by Pope John initiated the Church into a process of self-criticism, dialogue and transformation, from which she may never totally escape. The immutable Church may be forever a thing of the past. The christian Church is a dynamic community open to God's Word and the needs of the world. Faithfully responding to the divine Word in the changing cultural environment of modern life, the Church will remain a community perpetually called to new life and to new forms of life. While at one time we may have regarded the immutability of the Church as a reflection of her divine origin, today we see in her resourcefulness and creativity a sign that her mission is more than human. By her very nature the Church is on the move.

The changing Church poses a problem to the abiding character of the christian faith. Many people are troubled by the changes going on in the life and teaching of the Church. They wonder how they can still cling to the unchanging truth of the christian faith. The Church has affirmed that in Jesus Christ God revealed himself once and for all and that the faith witnessed by the apostles and handed on in their community is the norm of truth for ages to come. This faith, once and for all delivered to the apostolic Church, cannot change. Jesus Christ remains the same, yesterday, today and tomorrow. For some people this central christian conviction is being

9

threatened today by the changes going on in the Church. Therefore, we must ask the question: What constitutes the abiding nature of the christian faith?

There was a time, not long ago, when theologians explained the abiding nature of the faith in terms of the unchanging creed. The teachings of the Church are immutable. In the theological tradition of the West we developed a highly conceptual or intellectual understanding of faith: faith tended to be understood as the acknowledgment of the divine teachings proposed by the Church. A man had true faith when he accepted the teachings of the Catholic Church. Faith tended to be looked upon as something that happened in the human intellect: on the authority of God, mediated through Christ and his Church, the believer integrated new truths into his intellectual life, truths about God and human redemption, truths that could not be demonstrated, that transcended nature, that were accepted solely on divine authority. Faith was the acknowledgment of the Church's teaching as divine truth.

One should add immediately that the great theologians of the past always presented a more profound understanding of faith. For the great theologians of all ages, even when they adopted a highly conceptual understanding of faith, faith was always a salvational reality, the action of God in the human heart, and hence the beginning of everlasting life. Nonetheless, throughout many centuries, theologians were primarily concerned with the conceptual character of faith. Wrestling against false teachings which threatened the Church from many sides, faith tended to be looked upon more and more as the acceptance of the articles of the creed and all authoritative teaching. Faith was unchanging because the Church's teachings were unchanging.

Because of this heritage, the changing Church of the present day poses grave problems to the abiding nature of christian faith. Fortunately—and inevitably—the changes in the Church have modified and deepended the understanding of faith. Through biblical studies and ecumenical dialogue, through the influence of personalist philosophy and a new experience of the liturgy, the Catholic understanding of faith has been somewhat transformed over the last decades. This new theological approach has been endorsed and promoted by the documents of Vatican II. The deeper understanding of faith will enable us to solve the present difficulty.

The concept of faith has been deepened according to two dimensions, which we shall refer to as "personal" and "universal". Since this deeper understanding of faith is well-known in contemporary theology and since it has already influenced the new approach to catechetics and religious education in general, I shall confine myself to a very brief explanation of these two dimensions.

The "Personal" Dimension of Faith

Faith involves the whole person. In faith man does not accept truths about God, but in faith man responds to the living God who addresses him in his Word. God's Word, revealed in Christ and preached by the Church, summons man and evokes in him the response of faith. In contemporary literature, faith is often described as a personal encounter with God in Christ. What happens to man is not the introduction to new truths about God and his plan of salvation, but an encounter with God's living Word which transforms him, creates faith in him and establishes him in a new living relationship with God. Contemporary authors in no way deny that this encounter has a conceptual or intellectual component, and hence, that it can be expressed in words; but they insist that the intellectual content of faith must be understood in

the wider context of the total reality of faith, which is man's
Spirit-created response to the divine Word.

The "Universal" Dimension of Faith

The second dimension in which the understanding of
faith has grown may be called "universal". Contemporary
theologians have tried to describe the gift of faith in terms
which reveal that this gift is also available beyond the Church's
preaching. Abraham was a believer long before the creation of
a covenanted community and a message of salvation. Abraham, the father of faith, was summoned by God to leave his
family and enter upon a new future as yet unknown to him;
and the response to this summons in trust was the faith that
justified him. While the apostles, especially Paul, insisted that
Christ is the only mediator of saving faith, they also affirmed
that the faith which Christ creates in the Church is the same
saving reality that was present in Abraham and in the faithful
Israel. It should be possible, therefore, to describe this reality
in terms that are more universal than those of the creed.

In our age the conviction has grown in the christian
Church, strongly endorsed by Vatican II, that salvation is
offered to men wherever they are. Since faith is the beginning,
root and foundation of all justification, we conclude that the
divine Word, incarnate in Christ, is in fact addressing all
men. Theologians must, therefore, explain what faith could
mean in people who have not heard the Gospel. What is the
saving faith available to men beyond christian preaching?
Since there is a single way of salvation, namely, Jesus Christ,
the faith to which men are summoned outside of the Church
must be essentially the same as that created by Christ's message
in the Church. To show that such an assertion makes sense,
contemporary theologians have given an account of christian

faith in terms that also apply to secular people in the ordinary situations of their lives. The above remark that Abraham was summoned to leave his mother and father to enter upon a promised future as yet unknown to him, suggests that a secular description of faith is neither difficult to produce nor foreign to the intention of the scriptures.

Deeper Understanding of Divine Revelation

This understanding of faith expanded according to the two dimensions, personal and universal, was acknowledged by Vatican II. The significant document to be studied in this connection is the *Constitution on Divine Revelation*. A remarkable doctrinal shift occurred in the writing of this document.[1] After a long discussion and some heated controversy, the Council adopted a concept of divine revelation that went far beyond the traditional one. From understanding revelation as divine doctrine the Council passed to the understanding of divine revelation as God's self-communication to his people. God does not reveal truths about himself; in divine revelation God discloses himself. Revelation is self-revelation. Through historical acts and the prophetic Word accompanying them, God manifests himself to the people of Israel until, at the moment chosen by him, he reveals himself unconditionally and definitively in the person of Jesus Christ. In the christian Church this self-communication of God in his Word continues. The witness to the divine self-revelation in Christ has been once for all delivered to the apostolic Church and cannot be supplemented: this is what it means to say that revelation is closed. But from another point of view, revelation continues. God continues to speak his self-same Word in the Church. God

[1] See G. Baum, "Vatican II's Constitution on Revelation: History and Interpretation", *op. cit.*

continues to create the Church as the community of believers through his own self-communication in his Word. The Word, incarnate in Jesus, proclaimed by the Church and addressing Christians today, evokes the Spirit-created reality of faith in the community, making it the community of the faithful.

This deeper understanding of revelation implies a concept of faith that acknowledges its personal and universal dimensions. What is this personal dimension? Since God makes himself known in his Word, faith is the personal response to the divine Word. And what is the universal dimension? Since the God who discloses himself definitively and unconditionally in Jesus Christ, has communicated himself, provisionally and conditionally, to all men from the very beginning of human history right to the present, the response of faith, fully spelled out only in the Church, exists beyond the Church in the whole of humanity.

This concept of divine revelation enables us to deal with the problem raised at the beginning of this chapter: How can we affirm the abiding faith in a Church that is perpetually on the move? How can we assert the unchanging self-identity of faith even if the doctrine of the Church should undergo development? The answer is that faith is the faithful acknowledgement of God's self-revelation. Faith is an abiding self-identical reality in the Church—and in this sense unchanging —because it is the Spirit-created response to the divine Word. *The unchanging truth of the christian faith is the self-communication of God to his people.*

FAITH AS NEW CONSCIOUSNESS

Until now our remarks have been somewhat abstract and technical. To speak of God's self-communication in faith has a touch of unreality about it. It seems to suggest that faith is a rare, other-worldly occurrence granted to the great mystics. Calling faith an encounter between God and man or a dialogue of God's Word and man's response, seems to take us out of the sphere of ordinary human experience. When we described faith as the acknowledgment of doctrines, this at least was a concrete way of speaking. Everyone knew what this meant. It was easy to think of examples of what we believe in. The deeper understanding of faith has introduced us to beautiful language about divine self-disclosure without, apparently, making clear to what ordinary, concrete experiences this language refers. To speak about God's self-communication to man in his Word has a high-sounding tone. In the following pages I wish to describe—though by no means exhaustively—what this divine self-revelation means, or could mean, in concrete terms.

God Is Father

Christians go to church on Sunday morning to hear the Good News. We are being told again that God is Father; and since there is power in the proclamation of the Word, we come to believe again that God is Father. Throughout the week we often react quite differently in regard to God. We sometimes think of him as the distant cause of the world, or the heavenly ruler of the universe, or the severe judge constantly watching us, or a nebulous something or other with little reality. But on Sunday morning we hear again, and come to believe again, that God is Father. The author of reality is on our side. The ground of being is not far away, hostile or indifferent to us: the deepest dimension of the total reality facing us is for us. There is no reason to be afraid of the world; there is no reason to fear the unknown tomorrow; for the ultimate root of all being protects and favors human

life. Despite the suffering and evil in the world and the flood
of injustice in human history, we are summoned to believe
that the ultimate principle of reality is love itself. There is
meaning and purpose in the universe. There is meaning and
purpose in our lives. We are not handed over to the destructive
powers present in the world; we believe that we are set into
a context where growth and protection are available to us.
God is for us. God is Father.

What happens to us, or may happen to us, on Sunday
morning is that God speaks to us in power. He makes himself
known to us. Through the proclamation of the Church he
discloses himself to us—thereby creating a living faith in us.
We have here a concrete example of what divine self-communication means. Coming to believe in God as Father
induces in us a transformation of consciousness; we are
sustained by trust; we abandon some of our fears; we face
reality with courage; we regain a sense of purpose.

We note that there is a considerable difference between
professing the faith of the Catholic Church that God is Father
and believing that God is Father. It is quite possible for us
to acknowledge the doctrine that God is Father and yet really
believe that God is against us, that he is a judge making us
uncomfortable or a king ruling human life from afar. To
believe we must be converted. A personal transformation is
necessary. Something must happen to us if we are to believe
that God is Father; this "something" is the divine self-communication. This life-creative self-disclosure of God is present
above all in the proclamation of the Good News and the
celebration of the sacraments.

From this practical example we learn that faith cannot
simply be equated with the acknowledgment of doctrine. I
can firmly hold the doctrine that God is Father and yet not
really believe that God is Father. We note, however, that,
if I do believe that God is Father, then the doctrine that God

is Father gives authentic witness to my faith. If we speak about our faith, we inevitably express ourselves in doctrinal symbols and formulas. Because of the distinction between holding a doctrine and believing what it signifies, we must conclude that faith is not the addition of new truths to the human intellect; faith is, rather, a transformation of human consciousness. Believing that God is Father changes the way we experience life. We acquire a new awareness of ourselves and of our relationship to the reality facing us. The faith evoked by the divine self-communication profoundly modifies man's consciousness.

This is an important point in the development of this chapter. Faith creates in us a new consciousness. The faith that God is Father modifies our self-experience and our orientation toward the world surrounding us. For this reason it should be possible to describe this faith by giving an account of the new human consciousness. One should be able to translate the faith that God is Father into terms taken from man's self-awareness. Instead of describing this faith with reference to the God who reveals himself, we should be able to describe it with reference to the new self-consciousness which the divine Word creates in us. We should be able to talk about divine faith in human terms.

Such an endeavor may sound a little startling. We believe, after all, that faith opens a man to divine transcendence. In faith a man is delivered from the confines of his own existence and passes beyond himself to the One who approaches him in grace. This transcendental dimension of faith is its very essence. In faith man is in touch with the divine reality beyond himself and the entire created world about him. Yet since this transcendental orientation creates a new consciousness in man, it should be possible to describe this faith in God in terms taken from human self-awareness. To affirm, therefore, that faith in God can be equivalently translated and expressed as a new state of human consciousness in no way belittles the transcendent character of faith.

What does this mean in practical terms? To believe that God is Father is to believe that I am son. God's self-communication to me as Father initiates me into a new consciousness of myself as son. Who am I? Do I think of myself as isolated? as exposed to the coincidences of every day? as placed in a universe without meaning and without a future? There are indeed moments in my life when I experience myself in this way. There are times when I fear that I have no destiny. There are times when it seems to me that the only destiny I have is that which I create myself, by my own feeble efforts, wrestling in a hostile world; and this overwhelming task either makes me compulsive in my endeavors or pushes me into depression and inactivity. Yet the message that God is Father evokes in me the faith that I am son. Faith means to believe that I have a destiny. I do not have to create this destiny by my own efforts: it has been given to me. In faith I acknowledge it. I understand myself as placed in a context where meaning and purpose are available to me. The web of interconnectedness, to which I belong, offers me growth and the possibility of sharing with others. This destiny makes me someone. In faith I acknowledge my own worth; not because of the efforts I have made, but because as a son I am accepted. In faith there is no reason for me to be ashamed of myself. As son I rejoice in myself.

To believe that God is Father is to believe that I am son. It is important to reflect on this. For there is a certain ascetical tradition in Christianity which tends to create in men such exaggerated guilt feelings and such a dissatisfaction with themselves that they find it difficult to believe that they are sons. A severe moralism can make people so restless that they are unable to accept themselves in faith. They cannot relax in the knowledge that they are who they are. These people feel that they must perform a series of acts before they can be at peace with themselves; and when they have done them all, they create new obligations for themselves by which to condition their self-acceptance. The saving message that God is Father evokes the faith in us that we are sons. God is on our side. Not that this faith approves the sinful and destructive in us! As we believe that we are sons, the burden of sin is lifted and we become able to wrestle more effectively with the powers of self-destruction in us.

God's self-communication, as mediated by christian preaching, initiates men into a new self-consciousness. Divine revelation discloses man unto himself. A man cannot come to self-knowledge by looking at himself: he must be told who he is by another. In the Gospel God reveals to us that we are sons: we are led to acknowledge ourselves as people with a destiny, placed in a context of meaning, possessing ourselves in peace.

Using the same example of God revealing himself as Father, I wish to show that faith also creates a new orientation toward the world in which we live. What is the world to me? How do I react in regard to it? Do I regard the world as a chaotic reality where sin and injustice rule and brute power alone is able to assert itself? Do I regard the world as people competing with me or hostile to me? When I ask this question I do not look for a speculative answer. I may well speculate about the world according to various theories. Yet, what I want to find out is how I react in regard to the world; what it signifies to me in the concrete experience of life; how I respond spontaneously to the human environment. By looking at my actions, my feelings and my spontaneous thoughts, I discover who I am to myself and what the world is to me. We realize very well that we are not free, on the strength of our will power, to change our attitude to reality. A transformation of a man's basic orientation to reality is possible, but it is never the result of will power. Something must happen to men that initiates them into a new orientation to the world.

What, then, is the world to me? Is it a place of hostility, or is it a place where friendship is possible? Do I experience the world as a single human family, wounded indeed by sin and hence involved in awful crimes, yet orientated toward growth and reconciliation? Are other people threats to me, or do I respond to them as brothers? Am I sensitive to the marvelous things that do happen in the world of men, despite their sins? The man of faith sees in these marvelous things signs of the fellowship that is offered to men and that constitutes their destiny. Despite the awful crimes that are being committed and the exploitation inflicted on large sections of the human family, the man of faith believes that history has a meaning. Do I react to the world practically and concretely with the conviction that a salvation history has been appointed for it, or do I despair of the world? The basic orientation to the world surrounding us, which is part of human consciousness, largely determines how we act, how we think and make our choices. *It shapes our political involvement.* These remarks explain what is meant by the affirmation that God's self-revelation proclaimed by the Church initiates men into a new orientation to the world. To believe that God is Father means to believe that men are destined to be brothers and that salvation is at work in their history. God revealing himself as Father discloses to us the salvational meaning of history and thus changes our basic orientation to the world surrounding us. This is the political aspect of divine revelation.

In the preceding pages I have tried to show the ordinary, down-to-earth meaning of the high-sounding expression "God's self-communication". By reflecting on the message that God is Father, we have seen that God's self-communication revealed in power, transforms man's self-consciousness and his world-orientation and that it is possible, therefore, equivalently to express the faith in God as Father as an entry into a new self-awareness—"I am son"—and into a new experience of the world—"We are a family".

God Is Word

Let us take another example of divine self-revelation. As we go to church on Sunday morning, we may hear the message that God is Word. God is always Word. He always speaks. In whatever situation a man may find himself, by whatever problems he is challenged, it is the Church's faith that he is being addressed by God and summoned to salvation. This is Good News. We often think of God as mute; we tend to think of him as being far away, unconcerned or silent in regard to the problems that beset us. Sometimes we feel that we must rely on our own wisdom to extricate ourselves from difficulties. But the christian message says that God is always Word. God always addresses man: he is his own speech to us. The summons to new life is omnipresent to human life.

The Word of God, the Church proclaims, has become flesh in Jesus Christ. God addresses us in Jesus. Jesus is his message to us, his definitive and unconditional self-communication. Jesus is the divine Word. The Christian hears in Christ the divine summons to be converted and enter new life; he hears in Christ the Word that formulates his deep questions about life and utters the redemptive reply to them; he hears in Christ the meaning God offers to every human life. In Christ he learns that God summons men to become more truly human. The divine summons humanizes man. Man is called into death and resurrection in order to enter more deeply into the new humanity revealed in Christ.

Again we note that there is a great difference between

confessing the teaching of the Catholic Church that God is Word and believing that God is Word. It is possible to accept the creedal statement that God is Word and yet not really believe that God summons one in every situation. It is possible to say that God is Word and yet despair that he does not speak. Faith is more than accepting doctrine. Faith transforms human consciousness. The divine self-communication as Word initiates men into a new relationship to God. According to the preceding remarks, we may add that this self-communication creates a new self-awareness in man and orientates him in a new way to the world in which he lives. What does this mean concretely?

To believe that God is Word means to believe that man is a listener. We cannot come to self-knowledge by ourselves. We have to be told who we are by another. If we try to come to self-knowledge simply by reflecting on ourselves, we might be tempted to define ourselves simply in terms of our own resources. We might understand ourselves simply in terms of human nature. But man cannot be defined simply in human terms. Man, it is revealed to us, is always a listener. He is open to the truth that leads to life. In whatever situation he may find himself, he is open to the summons addressed to him, the summons that leads to growth and reconciliation. This is the Good News. A man who experiences himself as a listener will enter every conversation, every human relationship, every manifestation of human art and wisdom, with the readiness to discern the voice that calls him to greater self-knowledge and strengthens him to grow in his humanity.

There is much in us that is afraid of truth. Truth unsettles us. Something in us prevents us from being listeners. We have positions to defend and privileges to cling to, we entertain our own selfish plans: these prevent us from listening. We do not want to be told the truth. We do not want to be summoned to the knowledge of reality. We prefer to live with the illusions we have created for ourselves. The transition from not wanting to listen, to the new self-awareness of being a listener is the marvelous transformation produced by God's self-communication to us as Word. To believe in God as Word is to acknowledge myself in faith as a listener. If divine revelation makes me a listener, I am able to leave the confines of my own wisdom, listen to the message present in my daily experience and be open to the meaning hidden in the life that surrounds me. The world in which I live is no longer silent: my ears are open to the summons that creates new life.

To believe that God is Word means to trust that wherever a man may be, he is being summoned by God. But what is this summons addressed to him? What message will he hear as he becomes a listener? As Christians we believe that the summons addressed to men everywhere is spelled out in Jesus Christ. This message is death and resurrection as the passage to new life. Wherever a man is, he is summoned to come to self-knowledge, to recognize in himself the self-destructive tendencies, to face the inner bonds that prevent him from being truly human: but this same summons also evokes a new freedom in man, enabling him to die to the self-destructive drive in himself and to rise to a new dimension of love and concern. Man is summoned to conversion. Man is called to turn away from the death to which he clings, to the new life of which he is still afraid. The content of the Word addressing man, is Jesus Christ.

Faith in God as Word can be equivalently expressed as the initiation into a new self-consciousness: to believe that God is Word is to believe that I am a listener. Here again we see that a witness to God's self-revelation can be translated into a witness about human life—a human life in which God is involved. Following our line of thought, we want to show that this faith can also be expressed as a new orientation to the world. The faith that God is Father, we said above, makes us experience the world of men as a family appointed to salvation. To believe that God is Word, in fact Word made man in Jesus Christ, is to look upon the world as a family of men, affected by sin, yet ever summoned to new life, in whose midst the christian Church has been called forth as the community proclaiming Jesus Christ.

The faith that God is Word specifies a new orientation to the world. Believing that God is Word creates a new relationship to other people since it means acknowledging that the mystery of death and resurrection alive in oneself also addresses other men. It creates a new relationship to the whole world of men since in Jesus Christ God has adopted the human race as his people, to which he is present as his life-giving Word and into which the Church has been sent as messenger of truth and unity. This orientation to the world, I repeat, is not a speculative thing: I am here dealing with the basic orientation of life which is the source of our spontaneous reactions. Who are other people to me? What is the human community to me? How do I relate myself to the forces in history that divide man against man, and how do I relate myself to the movements that seek to reconcile people in a unity that permits the growth of all? These basic attitudes precede our intellectual reflections: they are constitutive of who we are as persons. The orientation to the world as a family of men, summoned to growth and reconciliation, is the creation of God's self-communication to us as Word become man. This world-orientation is faith.

God Is Spirit

Let us move on to a third example of divine self-communication. As we go to church on Sunday morning, we hear the saving message that God is Spirit. The Gospel proclaimed in power evokes in us the faith that God is alive in us and in others as Spirit. We come to believe more firmly that God is not only the author of reality who is for us (Father), God is not only the inexhaustable and unconditional meaning summoning us to new life (Son), God is also alive in us and in others as the source of growth and creativity (Spirit). God, we are told, is not only the creator facing us, he is not only the call that humanizes us, he is also present in us creating life out of death.

This message is Good News. For we often feel that we are half-dead. We often fear that we are totally determined by our own inner resources. We dread that the limitations and compulsions of our inner life will determine our future. Tomorrow, we fear, will be simply what we have made it ourselves. The new will not happen: we are trapped in the closed universe of cause and effect. The message that God is Spirit evokes the faith that a mystery of new life is present in me and in others. My future is not totally determined by the foolish things I do today. The new really happens. There is forgiveness of sins. It is possible to leave behind the ties that bind us to the past. The decisive break with old patterns and the possibility of new responses are available to us. There is an inexhaustible creativity alive in me, and in others, so that tomorrow will be different from today. Man is not trapped in the world: God as Spirit is at work in men producing the new creation.

This faith that God is Spirit can again be equivalently expressed as initiation into a new self-consciousness and a new orientation to the world. To believe that God is Spirit is to believe that I am alive, alive not by my own limited and even deformed resources, but alive by a principle that transcends me, over which I have no power, but that has power over me. This is Good News. For we often feel more dead than alive. We often think that we are just what we are now and other people are just what they are now. We fear that there is no possibility of newness. But God's self-communication as Spirit creates in us a new self-awareness. We believe that man is always more than man. There is a principle operative in man that transcends him. We are alive, and other people are alive, thanks to a mystery that takes place at the core of our being, offering new life, giving courage, producing growth, making us capable of love, stimulating new ideas, creating insight, calling life out of death. Faith evokes in men the new consciousness that they are alive with a life that triumphs over death. Faith is the beginning of eternal life.

Faith in God as Spirit also initiates men into a new orientation to the world. In faith the world of men becomes the place where the mystery of redemption takes place. Because I believe in the Spirit, I see the world in a certain light and dedicate myself to transforming it. Faith in God as Father and as Word creates a new orientation to the human environment in which we live. The saving message that God is Spirit specifies this relation even more. Faith in God the Spirit acknowledges the mystery of new creation at work in the world. I am faithful to who I am only as I involve myself in the life of the community and serve this mystery as it takes hold and transforms men.

In the above pages I have tried to give a concrete and down-to-earth description of what theologians mean by the high-sounding phrase of divine self-communication. I have given three examples of this. They happen to be those that have become normative for the proclamation of the Gospel in the christian Church. Faith is abiding because it is man's openness and response to God's self-disclosure as Father, Word and Spirit. Faith is an abiding, self-identical reality and in this sense unchanging because of God's faithful, continuing gift of himself. We did not say, please note, that faith is an unchanging reality because God is unchanging or because

doctrine is unchanging. We have affirmed the unchanging
character of christian faith because of the self-identity of
God's on-going self-communication.

The above reflections have brought out, moreover, that
it is possible to translate faith in divine self-revelation as an
entry into a new self-conciousness and a new orientation
toward the world. This is a startling conclusion, the full
justification of which cannot be given in this chapter.[2] All we
have done is to translate faith in God, Father, Word and
Spirit, as the new self-awareness—evoked by God's self-
communication—of men with a destiny, of men who are
listeners and of men alive by a principle stronger than death.
In these terms it is easy to explain to people what we believe.
If we speak about "the most holy Trinity", we easily create
the impression that we talk about a God who is beyond human
life and occasionally related to it. If we use the language of the
creeds, we seem to make statements about what is far away
and removed from the problems of human existence. But
since divine revelation is not information about another
world but God's self-communication to man, and hence his
gracious entry into the dynamic process of man's becoming
fully human, it is possible to express what the Church believes
by describing the new self-consciousness created by faith.
This, as we have mentioned above, does not belittle the
transcendent character of faith. Through faith man is brought

---

[2] The full justification of this thesis demands a reflection on the
mystery of the incarnation. What is revealed in Jesus Christ is that
the God-for-us is the God-in-himself. Since, therefore, the presence
of God to human life and consciousness is, in fact, God as he is in
himself, it should be possible—even if not always desirable—to translate every statement about God into a statement about human life
and consciousness. This understanding of incarnation is at the heart
of Karl Rahner's theology and affects much of contemporary Catholic
theology. See K. Rahner, "Theology and Anthropology", *The Word
in History*, New York 1966.

in touch with the creative and redemptive mystery we call God. This encounter cannot be described as learning new truths about God. This encounter is redemptive, it transforms man, it relates him in a new way to the whole of reality and therefore creates a new human self-consciousness. To believe in God as Father, Word, and Spirit means to be initiated into the self-awareness—in the sense explained above—that we are people with a destiny, that we are listeners, and that we are alive beyond the power of death.

Understanding faith as the entry into a new self-consciousness, created by divine self-communication, enables us to express this faith in contemporary terms. It helps us, moreover, to become deeply convinced of its abiding character, even in a Church that changes in liturgical practice, ecclesiastical organization and doctrinal formulation. For throughout these changes, the Good News of God, Father, Son and Spirit enables us to face life as sons at peace with themselves, as listeners open to the new, and as men alive by a principle that creates life out of death.

We note, moreover, that this presentation of faith takes into account the two dimensions, personal and universal, which have been stressed by contemporary theology. A purely conceptual understanding of faith tended to equate faith with the acknowledgment of doctrine. The understanding of faith outlined in these pages presents faith as a transformation of man's self-awareness. The closest human model for the understanding of divine faith is the effect which certain human encounters have on us. Having met this remarkable person, having listened to him and believed him, my life has been profoundly changed: I understand myself in a new way; I experience the world in a different light. This is the human analogy, suggested in the scriptures themselves, which contemporary theologians use in the understanding of divine faith. Because God reveals himself to man in the proclamation of the Gospel, man's life is profoundly changed. The divine Word initiates man into a new self-consciousness.

The Universal Dimension of Faith and Unfaith

What about the universal dimension of faith? The above description of faith as new consciousness suggests that faith is produced by God's gift of himself not only in the Church, spelled out concretely in the life, death and resurrection of Jesus Christ, but also outside of the Church, wherever people are, implicit in the important experiences of their lives. Even irreligious people may come upon a self-awareness that hardly differs from that to which Christians are summoned. They may regard themselves as men with a destiny, they may be at peace with themselves, they may acknowledge with surprise that life has meaning, they may experience themselves as sons; they may also think of themselves as listeners, open to the new even when it is uncomfortable, ready to move wherever the summons leads them; they may also trust that they, and other people, are alive by a principle over which they have no power but which brings forth new life. When we meet such people we marvel. Simply by himself, relying on his own resources, man suffers from his isolation, from the burden of being himself, from the meaninglessness of life; simply by himself, man is trapped by the defenses that protect him from self-knowledge and uncomfortable truth; simply by himself, man becomes frightened by the death present in him, the power which he cannot escape. We marvel, therefore, when we meet people who have been delivered from this oppression. We marvel because as Christians we believe that theirs is the new consciousness produced by God's self-revelation to man. This happens explicitly and definitively in the proclamation of the Church, but since God is Word always and everywhere, this happens implicitly and provisionally wherever people are. Faith, divine faith, is the one basis for the humanization and reconciliation of man.

This presentation of faith also shows that unbelief is a death-dealing reality not only outside of the Church where people do not hear the Gospel but even in the Church where people hear and believe it. For what Christian would want to assert that he is totally surrendered to God's self-communication? Even in the believer there remains, as the deepest dimension of his sin, the resistance to God's gift of himself as Father, Son and Spirit. There are layers of mental life of which even the believer is still afraid and does not believe that God is Father; there are areas of his life where even he does not want to be a listener and acknowledge that God is Word; there are dimensions of his personality where even he is overwhelmed by his passivity and refuses to believe that God is Spirit.

The New Testament gives us a detailed description of unbelief in the resistance of Christ's contemporaries to his message. There we read of man's unwillingness to listen, to come to self-knowledge, to discover the flaws in his own ideals, to abandon his own self-image, to relinquish positions of privilege. There we read of the fierce desire to cling to the past, to hold on to defenses, to pretend that things are going well. Because man did not want to come to self-knowledge, discover himself as sinner and admit the need for redemption, he was unable to open himself to the message of the kingdom. A person who is totally overpowered by this unbelief excludes himself from human growth and the sources of new life: he elects death. But even the believer, even the man whose self-awareness is constituted by the divine self-disclosure, is not totally free from unbelief.

Unbelief is a reality in the Church.[3] For this reason the

[3] Cf J.-B. Metz, "Unbelief as a Theological Problem", *Concilium* (Glen Rock, N. J.: Paulist Press, 1965), Vol. 6, pp. 59-78.

Church and every single Christian remain in need of the Word. We remain in need of the liturgy in which faith is stirred up and strengthened. We remain in need of the scriptures through which the Word summons us. The proclamation of the Gospel reveals to us the hidden layers of our unbelief and creates in us successive conversions to the new life God offers us.

We conclude that Christians are closely united to the rest of mankind. The summons of life, openly proclaimed in the Church, addresses every man in a hidden way. Always and everywhere God is Father, Son and Spirit. The Gospel happens wherever people are. At the same time the power of unbelief, which kills life, is present not only in those men who have chosen to resist the saving Word, it exists also in the believers who open themselves to the divine voice. The Church is united to the human family in the gift of God which is God himself and in man's resistance to this gift which is unbelief. These are basic considerations which must determine the understanding of the Church's mission in the world.

DOCTRINE AS WITNESS

Until now we have spoken of faith in terms of God's self-disclosure to men. In these terms it is easy to show that faith is an abiding, self-identical and in this sense, unchanging reality. We now must ask the question how doctrine is related to this faith. Many difficulties Christians have in connection with their faith have to do with doctrine.

Doctrine is the Church's witness to God's self-revelation in Jesus Christ. The Church, the entire christian community, gives witness to God's on-going self-communication in his Word. Doctrine recalls and proclaims what God has done

and is doing in Jesus Christ. Doctrine points beyond itself to
the saving reality to which it testifies. Even though doctrine
refers to a reality that transcends it, it is strictly necessary.
Without doctrine we could not talk about the redemption
which is at work among us. Without doctrine we could not
communicate with one another and form a fellowship of faith.
Without doctrine we could not enter into conversation with
other people telling them how the God, who revealed himself
in Jesus Christ, is redemptively involved in the whole of
human life.

Catholics believe that the witness of the community, or
the formation of doctrine, is guided by the Holy Spirit. We
believe that God is present to the Church in the making of
her creed. When doctrine is "defined" by a process in which
the whole Church is involved, ultimately through bishops and
the pope, we often call it "dogma". In the usual terminology,
dogma is a witness to God's self-disclosure that has been
declared normative by the Church's teaching authority. In
this chapter we wish to clarify the difference between faith
and doctrine and by doing so resolve some of the difficulties
encountered by christian believers today.

First we want to establish the important distinction between doctrine and the divine reality to which it gives witness.
This distinction has not always been made. At the turn of the
century, during the period often called the modernist crisis,
this distinction was regarded as dangerous. The ecclesiastical
government thought that this distinction made doctrine a
relative thing and implied that even dogma can change.
Thanks to the advance of Catholic theology throughout this
century, it has become possible to make this distinction without threatening the definitive and unconditional character
of God's revelation in Christ. In his opening speech to Vatican
II, Pope John himself distinguished between God's revelation
in Christ and the formulation of this revelation in the Church.

While God's self-disclosure in Christ is final and exhaustive, the doctrinal witness to this truth could, if need be, undergo modification.[4]

The documents of Vatican II endorsed the distinction made by Pope John.[5] The Catholic Church declares that her dogma is true. Its formation is guided by God and hence infallible. Nonetheless true doctrine points beyond itself to a divine reality transcending it. True doctrine gives witness to, and thus mediates, the saving Word of God. It is important to stress that this saving Word, made concrete in Jesus Christ, transcends any and every doctrinal expression of it in the Church.

Theologians in the Scholastic tradition like to speak of "the truths of faith". Christ confided certain "truths" to the apostles, and the Church continues to teach these truths divinely revealed. The ecclesiastical documents have often adopted this terminology: they often refer to the truths of faith taught and defended by the magisterium. This terminology could be understood in a superficial manner. It could be made to imply that these truths are propositions about God and his plan of salvation and that saving faith is simply the acknowledgment of these divinely revealed truths. The great theologians of the Church have never spoken of faith in this way. Yet the expression, "the truths of faith", may be understood in a more profound manner. Truth, in this context, may be understood as salvational truth. It is truth that mediates the living God. It is truth that redeems man. It is truth that gives witness to and renders present the living Word of God. The truths of faith or the articles of faith are therefore, the

[4] "The deposit of faith is one thing, the way it is presented is another; for the truths preserved in our sacred doctrine can retain the same substance and meaning under different forms of expression" (AAS, 54 [1962] 792).

[5] Decree on Ecumenism, art. 6, Const. on the Church in the Modern World, art. 62.

authenticated testimonies of the Church to God's self-disclosure in Christ. The truths of faith are not propositions, the content of which can be drawn from an analysis of their terms. The truths of faith are propositions which reveal their significance only when placed into the context of the entire christian teaching and when listened to as testimonies to God's saving Word. Speaking of the truths of faith is, therefore, not objectionable as long as we entertain a salvational and not a rational understanding of truth.

Doctrine is the Church's witness to God's self-revelation. The role of doctrine in the Church is, therefore, ministerial. It serves the communication of the Word. It mediates divine salvation. Doctrine, morever, is conditional. It subtracts nothing from the truth of doctrine to insist that it is conditioned by the culture in which it is formulated and by the problems of the Church to which it responds. Doctrine is the witness of the Church, at a particular period of her history, to the self-identical, on-going revelation of God in Christ. Already in the New Testament we see that the various authors formulated their witness to the selfsame Christ in different ways, depending on the language they adopted, on the problems of the Churches for which they wrote, and on their own theological intention. Throughout her history the christian Church has formulated her witness to divine revelation as a reply to the controversies and problems in the christian community and in reliance on the linguistic and conceptual framework supplied by the culture in which it lived. Recent studies have brought out the significant change in the doctrinal witness of the Church as she passed from a Hebrew environment into the Hellenistic world. In a new cultural situation the Church testified to the ever self-identical divine Word in doctrinal formulas that corresponded to the language and the consciousness of the believing community.

There is an inevitable tension between doctrine and the

transcendent reality to which it gives witness. Doctrine can never exhaustively present the divine Word. Doctrine singles out a particular aspect of God's self-disclosure to men and clarifies it for the community. Since the Word transcends every expression of it in the Church, there is an inevitable tension between this Word and the true, though always partial and historically conditioned, doctrinal formulation of it in the Church. Though doctrine is strictly necessary for men on this earth who wish to have fellowship in the Gospel, doctrine is also a burden. It makes us impatient. Men become frustrated with the partial and historically conditioned character of doctrine. We desire greater immediacy and greater fullness. At the same time we realize that to abandon doctrine altogether would be to reject the Gospel as a principle of fellowship and universal reconciliation.

If the tension between doctrine and the reality it signifies becomes very great, the problems of faith are multiplied. If the doctrine of the Church replies to the questions of past generations and is expressed in a language no longer our own, it becomes very difficult for people to encounter through it the living Word of God. What is required in such a case is a more contemporary witness of the Church to God's self-disclosure in Christ. What is required is the reformulation of doctrine. Vatican II has called "the accommodation of preaching" to the exigencies of the present, "the law of all evangelization".[6]

In the present day the tension between the traditional doctrine of the Church and the divine reality which it signifies, has become very great indeed. We have become keenly aware that the language, the thought forms and often, the concerns of the scriptures are no longer our own. A few decades ago, a renewal movement in theology and catechetics supposed

[6] *Const. on the Church in the Modern World*, art. 44.

that the teaching of the Church could be made accessible to contemporary man by expressing it as much as possible in biblical terms. The liturgy, which is—in part, at least—the celebration of the scriptures, was regarded as the powerful Spirit-created instrument to communicate the Gospel to the present generation. Today we have become more conscious that the language of the bible, though more concrete and imaginary than the language of the creeds, is still far removed from the contemporary experience of reality.

The language of the patristic tradition of the Church is not our own. Our creeds are formulated in words which have changed their meaning. An amusing incident at Vatican II illustrates the change that has taken place. In the conciliar document on divine revelation, a proposed text affirmed that God revealed himself in the teaching, the life, death and resurrection of Christ, in brief, in the whole "person of Christ". Some bishops objected to this modern usage of "person". Person here obviously means what a man is and comes to be through his history. But, these bishops insisted, the faithful still use the word "person" in the ancient, metaphysical way to express the suppositum of a spiritual nature, as it was done in the christian creeds. When the faithful hear "person of Christ", they think of the eternal Word, the second person of the Holy Trinity. To honor the wish of these bishops, the final version no longer speaks of the "person" of Christ: the word is replaced by "manifestation and presence". What is amusing in this incident is that in the previous year, in the writing of the *Constitution on the Church,* the expression "person of Christ" in its modern sense had been approved by the entire Council.[7] We are so used to the language of our own culture that it takes a special effort to speak in another. When the *Constitution on the Church* said that the kingdom of

[7] *Const. on the Church,* art. 5.

God becomes manifest in the very person of Christ, the Council fathers spontaneously understood "person" in the modern sense and not one of them adverted to the fact that this usage deviates from the language of the creeds.

Since neither the biblical nor the Hellenistic language of the ecclesiastical tradition is our own, a great deal of scholarship is required to discern the meaning of the ancient terms. Taking these terms in their present meaning leads to a complete misreading of the Church's doctrinal witness.

The tension between traditional doctrine and the redemptive reality it signifies, is not simply a matter of changing terminology. As the Church moves into a new culture more changes than the language. What changes, above all, are the salvational questions people ask. Each culture is threatened in its own way. In each culture there are new possibilities of idolatry and new possibilities of redemption. Each culture poses its own crucial questions of life and death. The Church's traditional doctrine replies to questions which, in part at least, were different from the questions we ask today. This is what people mean when they say that the Church's preaching has become irrelevant. The recitation of the traditional creeds does not make divine revelation the Good News for today. Traditional doctrine gives witness to divine revelation in the context of issues that preoccupied people in a past age: it has little to say on the burning issues which trouble us today and in the context of which divine revelation must become Good News for us.

The tension between doctrine and the saving reality which it signifies, has become so great that the reformulation of doctrine has become imperative. In chapter 3 I shall show that the process of reformulating the Church's teaching was begun at Vatican II. The conciliar documents have shifted—or, at least, begun to shift—the focal point of the Gospel. The task of the contemporary Church is to re-interpret the traditional teaching in the light of this new focus.

CHRISTIAN DOUBT

Since there is a distinction between doctrine and the saving truth it signifies and mediates, it is possible for a man to ask the question whether he really believes in the God who discloses himself or whether he merely clings to the doctrinal formula. Do we really have faith? Do we acknowledge God's gift of himself to us in a new consciousness of ourselves and the world? Or do we simply, by force of custom, endorse a set of teachings? Do we know whether we pass beyond the doctrine to the saving reality which it signifies or whether we simply stop at the doctrine?

This question is not a new one. The medieval Scholastics raised the question whether a man can know the supernatural character of his faith. Some Scholastics thought that faith could be natural. It is possible, they thought, that a man assent to the teaching of the Church for reasons drawn from his own resources, from his own intellectual powers or his own emotional situation. Such a faith would not be saving. Faith initiates into justification only if it is the response to God's Word. Faith is justifying faith only if it is the redemptive gift of God to man. Can a man know, the Scholastics asked, whether he has justifying faith?

Today we analyze the possibility of a purely human faith in a different manner. We no longer think that a man could accept the christian teaching by the power of his reason reflecting on the divine origin of the Church. But we have learned that there are other purely human reasons, often hidden ones, why people might assent to the articles of faith.

It is possible to endorse the Church's creed from force of habit or tradition. It is possible to accept the truths of faith as a symbol for the unchanging social order which one desires. Belief can be a commitment to a conservative political program. Other people might accept doctrine as a symbol of protest against family and environment, or as a way of affirming a life of their own choice. Compulsions and hidden drives might make a man accept the teachings of the Church. The question that arises, therefore, with some anxiety is whether we can know if we really believe or whether we just compulsively cling to the formula. Are we really open to the mystery of God's self-communication or do we just hold a set of teachings? Are we really initiated by God into a new consciousness or have we lost ourselves in an ideological system?

The Catholic Church has given an answer to this question. No man *knows* whether he really believes! No man *knows* whether he stops at the doctrinal formula or whether he passes beyond the formula to the reality it signifies. The question arose at the Council of Trent in connection with a Protestant position—at least, as it was understood by Catholics then—proposing that to believe in Christ means to know that one has faith in him. Justifying faith comes about in us, the Reformers were understood as teaching, as we acknowledge Jesus Christ as our savior. To endorse the teaching of the Church is not enough: faith is the conscious acknowledgment that these teachings mediate the living Word to me and that I accept this Word as my judgment and my salvation now. From this follows that a man knows whether he believes. If he does not know whether he believes, he does not believe. Against this position—as they understood it—the bishops at the Council of Trent insisted that no man knows whether he is justified, no man knows whether he has received the justifying faith, no man knows whether his faith is grace-created

and grace-giving.[8] The conciliar text made an exception to
this. Because of the incidents in the New Testament where
Jesus told some men who trusted in him and were healed by
him, "Your faith has saved you", the conciliar text specified
that no man knows whether he has justifying faith, unless he
receives a special revelation. The position of the Council of
Trent is in keeping with the more general Scholastic principle
that the supernatural *qua* supernatural cannot be known. We
cannot know whether our belief is a purely psychological
reality or whether it is evoked by the living God summoning
us to new life.

To some people it may sound quite frightening to hear
that we can never know whether we really believe or only cling
to the formula. To others it may be a tremendous relief. For
this doctrine surely means that the key to the mystery of our
life is not in our own hands but in God's. As long as we live
in this earthly situation we can never completely know who
we are. We can only reach out for it. Our personal secret is
hidden in God. Faith is the only way to self-knowledge.

One must add here, still in line with Scholastic thinking,
that while we cannot know the supernatural character of what
happens to us, we must discern the signs by which God
accompanies his gift to us and through these signs come to
an estimate of where we stand. The signs that accompany the
faith that justifies are, according to St. Thomas, delight in what
is profound, indifference about what is superficial and the
peace of a good conscience.[9] In other words, it is our self-
awareness that permits us to estimate—not to know—that we

---

[8] "If anyone shall say that man is absolved from his sins and justified because he believes for certain that he is absolved and justified,
or that no one is truly justified but he who believes himself justified,
and by this faith alone absolution and justification are perfected, let
him be anathema" (Denz. 824).

[9] Cf. *Summa Theol.* I-II, 112, 5.

are the recipients of the divine self-disclosure. We can never be certain that our openness to the future, our willingness to listen and our trust in the mystery that unfolds within us is, in fact, salvational faith in God's self-disclosure: it might be induced by unconscious forces in us. According to Catholic teaching, there is no ultimate assurance of grace except God himself.

Because we do not know the inner hurdles in people's lives and do not understand our own, it may well happen that a man who is troubled by doubts and whose self-feeling seems to fall apart, has opened himself on a deep level to the divine self-communication and is a man of faith. We will never know from what abysses of self-destruction we are being saved by God. Even the fruitless struggle of a man to possess himself in a human way may be the result of God's presence in him, saving him from the horror of disintegration. Ultimately we cannot judge ourselves or other people. What we believe is that God is good and that man is never without the divine voice calling him to life.

Because of the tension between doctrine and the reality which it signifies, there is a restlessness at the heart of faith. The Christian must constantly reach out beyond the formula to the mystery. He is again and again confronted with the question of whether he simply clings to the inherited formula or whether he really believes the salvation the formula proclaims. He may often wonder whether he is in touch with the living Word that transcends him. Sometimes he may feel caged in by the articles of faith and have little awareness of the difference they make in his life and consciousness. How can we be sure that we pass beyond the doctrine to the life-giving self-communication of God?

Some people foolishly think that the less they think about the doctrines of faith, the easier it is for them to be believers. "Don't bother me with your questions," they seem to say;

"if I do not examine my beliefs, if I do not reflect on them, if I avoid embarrassing questions, then I can just make it. I have packed away my belief safely. If I unpack it and look at it, it might possibly disappear." Such an attitude does not protect the gift of faith at all. For such a person will have no assurance whatever that he reaches beyond the doctrinal statement to the divine reality it proclaims.

To pass from the doctrine to the saving Word we must be engaged in an inner dialogue. The only assurance we have that through the doctrine we come in touch with divine revelation is to keep on asking questions to which the Word of God gives the answers. The questions we ask are not of an academic nature: they are not abstract questions learned from a book. Life itself and our reflection on it supply us with current questions, salvational questions, to which God has promised to reply in his Word. Human life gives rise to an endless inner conversation. Some days we may be deeply impressed by the evil in the world and the hatred among men, and this raises questions; on other days we marvel at the nourishment that comes through friendship and we ask how this is related to salvation. Christian problems arise in connection with the divisions of mankind, the race conflict, overpopulation, the new situation created by technology and automation, the generation gap, etc. The ordinary person in touch with life will have many questions which he submits to the Word of God and for which he seeks solutions in the direction indicated by the christian message. This inner dialogue, which is by nature unending in this world, is the best assurance we have that we do not cling compulsively to a creed but open ourselves to the divine revelation to which the creed testifies.

The Role of Doubt in Faith

I now want to make a point to which I attach some significance. In the inner conversation, making us reach beyond the formula to the reality, it is inevitable that doubts will occasionally occur. It is important today to have an understanding of the life of faith, in which we are able to assign a place to doubts. In the past, when theologians tended to identify revelation and doctrine and, consequently, to reduce faith to the acknowledgment of divine truths, they had to look upon the doubts of the believer as acts directly opposed to the gift of faith and hence as gravely sinful and destructive of the supernatural life in its root. This theological teaching made Catholics so afraid of their doubts and sometimes even of their questions, that they were often unable to clear up the difficulties of faith, associated with growing up and becoming mature believers. Catholics can be so afraid of their doubts that they shy away from the painful process of passing beyond their childhood faith to acquire the faith of an adult. Since to be human means to be involved in growing, in seeking greater maturity, in finding more authentic ways of expressing and living one's faith, it is quite inevitable that doubts occur in the life of the sensitive Christian. The distinction between doctrine and the revelation to which it refers, enables us to explain the place doubts have in the life of faith.

On a previous page we have dealt with unbelief, which is man's death-dealing opposition to God's self-communication to him. Unbelief is the strict contrary of faith. We have shown that this sort of resistance to the divine gift exists not only outside the Church, in people whom we often call non-believers; it exists also in the christian Church. A certain unbelief exists in every believer; for even if a man acknowledges God's revelation evoking in him new consciousness, there remain some layers of his personality where he closes himself off from the divine gift and refuses to be led into new life. In some people this resistance to revelation determines the entire orientation of their lives: their unfaith excludes them from growth in the new life offered to them. They have chosen death.

Doubt, in our analysis, is quite different from unbelief. Doubt has to do, not with God's self-communication, but with the doctrines that give witness to it. Doubts will occur in a man's life of faith. It is inevitable that in the inner dialogue which assures us that we reach beyond doctrine to the reality it signifies, some questions arise with which we cannot deal, which place a question mark behind a dogma of the Church or even make questionable the very effort of listening to God. It is impossible to avoid all doubts. The only way to do this would be to stop the inner questioning by which we seek contact with the living Word. It is an ironic truth that if we are too frightened of doubts and thus refuse the inner conversation to which we are summoned, we may eventually cease to be believers altogether. The Christian is not overwhelmed by his doubts. He believes that God is Word, and hence, even if he should have doubts in regard to the Church's message, for which no answer is available today, he trusts that the God who is Word will provide an answer tomorrow. The doubts will pass. The summons of God will resolve the doubts and make deeper the faith in his self-communication.

I wish to analyze a little further the doubts that come to Christians in the inner conversation through which they listen to God's Word. A doubt comes to us at times suggesting that we are not in touch with any saving reality at all. We cling to the teachings of the Church, but we wonder if we pass through them to the living truth they are meant to express. Are we in touch with anything beyond ourselves? We fear sometimes that we have elevated to divinity the doctrines of the Church, themselves. Instead of worshipping God, we worship the doctrines that are meant to testify to him. Since doctrines are essentially ministerial and relational, to make an absolute of them would be idolatry. We wonder sometimes whether we have not fallen into a prison of words and ideas. Are we in touch with a saving mystery beyond us? Is there anyone that speaks to us? Is there God?

This sort of doubt need not be generated by the deadly power of unbelief in man; it may be evoked by the dynamics of faith itself. Divine revelation makes us critical; it makes known to us the ambiguity of all aspects of human life including religion. We are summoned to subject to the Word of God even our religious convictions. Is the divinity we worship really the God who has spoken in Christ or is it a deceptive god of man's own making? The scriptures tell us that man is an idolmaker. Man is always tempted to elevate to divinity what he cherishes. He always proves for himself the existence of some god. The Christian must ask himself whether the divinity he acknowledges is really the true God. He reads in the Epistle of St. John that if a man does not love his neighbor, he does not know God. If a man does not include all men in his love, the divinity he confesses is not the true God at all. The recitation of the creed alone is no guarantee that we believe in the true God. We must submit our religion to the judgment and the pardon of God's Word.

Since the scriptures teach that man, in his sinfulness, is an idolmaker, the Christian must consider the possibility that he has made the Church's dogmatic system an absolute and substituted it for the true God. We are tempted to worship our knowledge of the divine mystery instead of the divine mystery itself. By the inner dynamics of his faith the Christian is again and again brought to the question whether he endorses the christian creed as an absolute (and hence locks himself into the prison of idolatry) or whether he is really open to the self-communication of the true God to which the creed testifies. This sort of questioning inevitably brings him, at certain moments of his life, to the doubt of whether he is in touch with any reality beyond his own concepts. Are we really in touch with the saving mystery? Are we being spoken to, or do we simply listen to our own thought? Is there God?

While such doubt is painful, we see that it has a positive role in the life of faith. According to the scriptures man is a mythmaker. He is always ready to believe too much. His sin makes him uncritical. He is only too willing to add his own superstitions, his legends and his projections to the divine message. Man is tempted to be credulous and to acknowledge as divine what is not divine at all.[9] Man is tempted to transform the Gospel of Christ into a culture religion which approves the ideals of his society and condemns the attitudes that criticize or undermine it. Because we tend to make for ourselves a harmless or a deadly religion, we are summoned by God's Word to be critical. The Gospel saves us from credulity. The doubts we have, therefore, subject our beliefs again and again to the test of the Word and deliver us from the tendency to believe too much. To live with an unanswered question can be more in line with divine faith than to cling frantically to an answer which no longer satisfies our critical spirit.

Needless to say, no one advocates doubts as a good thing. Man is threatened on all sides. He is also tempted to be skeptical, to be suspicious of others, to be mistrustful, to expect the worst. Not to be able to believe other people is a vice. For this reason divine faith is threatened on both sides, by that in us which tends to believe too much and by that in us which is frightened of believing altogether. We can become so critical that we destroy, by reflection, the good things that

[9] Cf. L. Dewart, *The Future of Belief*, New York, 1966, pp. 123-24.

happen in our lives. Doubts which spring from this over-critical spirit are certainly destructive.

We do not advocate doubts. But the inner conversation through which we listen to God's Word inevitably leads us to some doubts and these doubts, though painful and not without danger, have a positive role in the life of faith.

At times Christians doubt whether doctrine brings them in touch with a saving reality; but there is another kind of doubt. We sometimes doubt whether doctrine is true. Does a particular doctrine express divine revelation? Does this doctrine recorded in the bible or that doctrine formulated by a council really give witness to the wonderful things which God has done and is doing in Christ? The Catholic believes that the Church is guided in the formulation of her doctrine, and hence, he tends to have confidence in her authoritative teaching dealing with the core of the Gospel. Yet, in the present age of critical research the Catholic is surrounded by many new questions.

Christian believers readily accept that scripture is the privileged record of God's Word. It is God's Word to us. And yet when we ask for the meaning of any particular passage in scripture, we turn to the exegetes and usually find that there is a variety of possible interpretations. The interpretation of biblical texts depends on how the scholar evaluates the meaning of language, the intention of the authors, and the spiritual climate of the community in which the texts were composed. These evaluations are worked out by the critical-historical method. But while many good reasons can be given for them, they cannot be demonstrated in the strict sense. Different assessments of these conditions lead exegetes to divergent conclusions. There is no scriptural interpretation without some presuppositions. The same thing happens today when we ask for the meaning of a particular doctrine defined by the Church. We turn to the historians of doctrine to learn that the council which defined this doctrine admitted several different interpretations of it. The theologians who preceded the council, we hear, understood this doctrine in slightly divergent ways and the council did not want to exclude any of these meanings from the life of the Church. The council only excluded extreme positions. Since a council defines doctrine in a particular situation of the Church, since it intends to reply to certain questions or resolve certain controversies, since it expressed itself in the language and in concepts taken from its own day, it is not easy to state what precisely in this doctrine is the witness to divine revelation and, consequently, what this doctrine means in the present age when the questions posed in the Church are so different. When we turn to theologians today to find out the exact meaning of a doctrine, we learn that there are a variety of interpretations, depending on the set of presuppositions with which they work, presuppositions which can be supported by excellent reasons but cannot be demonstrated. While Catholics accept the defined teaching of the Church, they do not agree on what these doctrines mean. To some they may have no meaning at all. How are we to interpret the meaning of biblical and ecclesiastical texts? This is the hermeneutical question.

We conclude from these remarks that the doubt expressed in the question: "Is this doctrine true?" today usually leads to the antecedent question "What does this doctrine mean?" Since this question is not easily resolved today, the question about the truth of doctrine has lost some of its urgency. Is the doctrine of the divinity of Christ true? Before we can deal with these questions, we must ask what these doctrines mean. In a later chapter we shall show that the meaning of doctrines in the Church is not a constant: to preserve the self-identity of the revealed Gospel, the Church must again and again reinterpret her teaching in order to make them the witness to God's Word addressed to men in the present. The abiding nature of christian faith and the unchanging reality which is the object of this faith, do not imply that the Church's doctrine is immutable.

II
A Modern Apologetics

In recent years interest in apologetics has decreased among Catholic theologians. One of the reasons for this lack of interest was the rediscovery of modern theology that God's Word is power. People come to believe in the Good News because the Word of God proclaimed by the Church, or rendered present in christian witness, has the power to move the heart and to evoke living faith. Thanks to the biblical and liturgical movements we have regained confidence in the power of the christian proclamation. We are deeply convinced that people come to believe, or come to believe more strongly, not because of cogent apologetical arguments but because of God's self-communication to them in the Gospel proclaimed and celebrated in the christian community. What is of primary importance, therefore, for the growth and development of the Church is to find ways of announcing the Gospel in a language that can be understood and to celebrate the gifts of Christ in a manner that makes sense to people of our age.

At the same time it seems to me that we cannot evade the apologetical question altogether. We must search for the *human* reasons why people believe. The divine reason for believing is God's powerful Word. God evokes faith in men as the response to his call. But since this divine gift of faith is also a fully human commitment, and hence free and responsible, we must inquire into the human reasons for believing. Why, humanly speaking, do people become Christians and why do they stay Christians?

51

19th-Century Apologetics

Let us first look at the apologetical approach of the 19th century, which has influenced Catholic religious literature until very recently. At the center of this approach was the radical distinction between faith and credibility. Faith is the divinely-inspired acceptance of the message. Faith is a gift. It cannot be demonstrated. Faith transcends the powers and the intelligence of the human mind. On this all christian theologians agree. But what is credibility?

For the 19th-century Catholic theologians the credibility of the faith was the divine origin of the message. Christian faith is credible or worthy of belief, they thought, because its divine origin can be demonstrated. It can be shown, they supposed, that the message of salvation, to be believed by the gift of faith, comes not from man but from God himself. But how can this be demonstrated? The 19th-century theologians used the following reasoning. The prophets, especially the greatest of prophets, Jesus Christ, uttered the message to be believed. Their utterances are available to us in the books of the scriptures. These prophets, the argument went, were reliable and trustworthy men. They were regarded as honest and upright even by the people who opposed them. They were not liars. Their holiness vouches for the authenticity of their message. If they insisted that the message they proclaimed came to them from God, they ought to be believed. These prophets, so the argument continued, supplied signs which demonstrated to their contemporaries and to people of later generations that their message was truly divine: they performed miracles and uttered prophecies. These miraculous happenings, recorded in the scriptures, are the proof that the prophetic message is indeed of divine origin. Miracles transcend human power. Men are bound to the laws of nature. Miracles indicate the presence of God. They are divine signs. Thanks to the miracles in Israel and especially, thanks to the miracles of Jesus Christ, we can demonstrate the divine origin of the christian message. The credibility of christian teaching, according to 19th-century apologetics, lies in the miracles of the scriptures, above all, in the miracles performed by Jesus Christ. Since the theologians of the last century regarded the gospels as reliable historical documents, giving a faithful report of what happened in the life of Jesus, they thought that on the basis of these documents the credibility of the christian faith could be demonstrated to all men, to Christians as well as to unbelievers.

The 19th-century apologists also sought to demonstrate the credibility of the christian message by reflecting on the Church as its teacher. The Church, they wished to show, proclaims a message of divine authorship. The Church announces a message of salvation, which she has not invented but received from the Lord of life. Are there signs, they asked, which vouch for the divine origin of the message? Yes. The 19th-century apologists thought there were miraculous signs in the life of the Church today, which vouch for the divine authorship of her message. Comparing the Church with other communities of men, the apologists sought to prove that the Church is altogether unique in her unity, her universality, her holiness and her continuity through the ages. Wherever people, sinful people, gather in a community we observe symptoms of disunity, signs of provincialism and partiality, manifestations of sin and a certain lack of continuity and stability. Only in the Catholic Church, these authors thought, are these universal manifestations of human failure—disunity, provincialism, sin and instability—marvelously overcome through the presence of the Spirit creating unshakable unity, world-wide catholicity, visible holiness and the continuity of apostolic succession. These four marks of the Church are, according to the 19th-century authors, miraculous signs vouching for the divine origin of the Church's message. The teaching of the Church is credible, according to this apologetical system, because the historical reality of the Church today has a transhuman, miraculous character demonstrable to believer and unbeliever alike.

Today this apologetical approach seems unsatisfactory to us. We do not find it as easy as previous generations to produce demonstrations for the arguments of credibility. The miracles of the scriptures and the miracle of the Church's present existence are not realities for us which we are willing to set up as arguments of rational appeal. If we do accept these marvelous happenings, it is rather because they fit into the vision of life which the christian faith has created in us. On the whole the radical distinction between faith and its credibility has been abandoned. We readily admit that a man discerns the credibility of the christian faith by the same élan of the mind by which he opens himself to the Word of God. The man who is being drawn to believe in the divine message becomes sensitive to the marvelous things that have happened in history, in his own history and that of God's people. The signs which the 19th-century apologists regarded as arguments of credibility may still be meaningful, but contemporary theologians insist that they have this meaning because a special inner disposition beyond pure rationality has opened men to their sign language.

In defense of the 19th-century theologians, it must be said that the radical distinction between faith and its credibility was a brilliant solution for dealing with two opposing tendencies, rationalism and fideism, which were regarded as threats to the Church at that time. A certain rationalist tendency sought to demonstrate the truth of the christian faith by a set of arguments of universal validity. A fideistic tendency, on the other hand, suggested that rationality had nothing to do with faith:

faith was a divine gift, and men came to accept it, not because it seemed rational to them but because it fitted into their lives and nourished their religious feelings. These two opposing tendencies—-as understood by the official theology—were condemned by the ecclesiastical magisterium. In dealing with these two tendencies, Catholic theologians invented the radical distinction between faith and its credibility. This enabled them to insist at one and the same time on the transcendental character of faith and on its rational foundation. Against the rationalists they asserted that faith is a divine gift, that it is not the conclusion of an argument, that it is never demonstrable; and against the fideists—as they understand them—they proposed that the credibility of faith, or the divine origin of the message, is capable of demonstration in the strict sense. With the fideists Catholic theology emphasized the gratuitous and transcendental character of faith and with the rationalists, it made much of the rational foundation on which this faith rests. In this way the Catholic theology of the 19th century sought to save the insights of two opposing tendencies, without giving in to their one-sidedness.

The Apologetics of Maurice Blondel

The approach to apologetics, based on the radical distinction between faith and credibility, was already attacked at the end of the 19th century by the great French philosopher and theologian, Maurice Blondel. In his *Letter on Apologetics* Blondel tried to show that this apologetical approach presupposes a false concept of divine revelation.[1] This approach implies that divine revelation has nothing to do with man's ordinary experience, that it is a message added to human life

[1] M. Blondel, *Letter on Apologetics and History of Dogma* (London, 1964).

from without, that it is offered as information about God and his plan for human life: the only reasons why this revelation is considered worthy of belief are the miracles associated with its proclamation. Blondel thought that this approach made divine revelation appear as a message from a foreign land, a cryptic utterance which does not fit into human life but for which room must be made artificially. Divine revelation appeared, according to this approach, as a statement that seems acceptable only on the strength of totally extrinsic arguments, drawn from the events accompanying the delivery of the message. This approach suggested that God might have revealed any sort of message at all, the more unlikely the better, as long as it was accompanied by miraculous events. It implied that the obedience of faith is a sacrifice of the intelligence: what seemed to count in believing God was the acceptance of an unlikely story, simply on the strength of his authority. This, Blondel thought, was a caricature of divine revelation and of the faith that saves.

It is not my intention to give a detailed presentation of Blondel's apologetical approach. The details of his method have not been followed by many Catholic thinkers, but his general approach has been acknowledged very widely. In this, and in other areas of theological reflection, Maurice Blondel has had a powerful impact on Catholic thinking. The presupposition of Blondel's apologetics is the redemptive presence of God to the whole of human life. God is involved where people are. He is present in their growth, in their aspirations, in their conversion away from destructiveness to love and in the extension of their responsibility to include the whole human family. Divine revelation in Jesus Christ, therefore, is not the addition of new knowledge to human life, introduced from another world; it rather clarifies and specifies the redemptive presence of God in the lives of men. The message of God uttered in Christ and handed on by the Church

reveals the hidden (supernatural) dynamism present in human
life everywhere. The message of salvation is not foreign to
human life, to be accepted simply on the strength of miracles.
The message of salvation ties into human life; it explains to
men what has been going on in their lives and what is their
destiny. The christian message makes known that the great
things that happen to people in the process of becoming more
human is the redemptive work of God in their lives. According
to the Blondelian approach, the christian preacher says to
people outside the Church: this is the christian message, you
listen to it, you try it on, you test it, it will explain to you
what has been going on in your life all the time. In Jesus
Christ you discover what it means to be human. The message
is not information about another world; it is the specification
of the divine summons that is gratuitously present in the lives
of all men, calling them to conversion, to growth, to reconciliation. Blondel named his approach the method of im-
manence.

An Apologetics for Our Own Day

In line with the Blondelian approach, I wish to develop an
apologetics for our own day which takes into account the
great variety of human gifts and talents, the diversity of human
experiences and the many values which people love and which
make them more human. People are different. The detailed
analysis of human action undertaken by Blondel, in which
man's yearning for the infinite plays a considerable role, does
not seem to apply to all people, especially in this secular age.
Some people become and stay Christians for one set of reasons
and others for another. The temptation of the theologian is to
reduce the human reasons for believing to a single system. In
the following I wish to present a flexible approach to apolo-

getics which leaves room for the differences among people
and the variety of human experiences.

According to my mind the study of christian origins does
not belong to apologetics. I do not think that people become
Christians or stay Christians because of the historical certainty
established by scholars in regard to the origin of the christian
message and the foundation of the Church. Today we no
longer look upon the scriptures as historical documents in a
modern sense; we have come to realize that it is difficult, if
not impossible, to draw a picture of the historical Jesus, to
reconstruct the details of his life and the content of his original
message. The gospels are confessional documents. They proclaim the faith of the early Church regarding the marvelous
things God has done and is doing in Jesus Christ. It is difficult
to know whether a saying of Jesus, recorded in the gospels,
goes back to his own ministry or whether it belongs to the
Church's post-Easter message. Moreover, as we read the
accounts of Christ's miracles, it is difficult to decide whether
they intend to record what actually happened in the life of
Christ or whether they simply adopt a traditional literary
device to announce that Jesus is the Messiah. Since the ancient
prophets foretold the coming of the Messiah in terms of the
new life God would create through him, symbolized by miraculous happenings, the evangelists may have proclaimed the
presence of Christ in Israel and his on-going glorious presence
in the Church in the same symbolic language. This is, at least,
a possibility.

At the same time the scriptures are not myth. In their own
way the scriptures give witness to history. They record the
marvelous events that created the people of Israel and within
that people, many centuries later, the coming of Christ, the
work of redemption and the formation of the christian community. The existence of the Jewish people and of the christian Church testify to the historical character of these great

events. The scriptural record is historical in a general sense, it declares what happened in the history of Israel, but it does not permit us to reconstruct the details of the story with precision.

The Church's witness to the historical character of the great salvational events is sufficient basis for Christians to reject the idea that the Gospel is a myth without foundation in history. In general the details are not important to people. Few people become Christians, or cease to be Christians, because the latest archeological discovery or the most recent theory of biblical criticism supplies new information regarding Christian origins. Whether the Fourth Gospel was written by an apostle, or by a disciple belonging to a later generation, whether it was written early in a Jewish-Christian context or later in a Gentile community is indeed important for the understanding of its message, but it is usually not an issue that makes people Christians or makes them give up their faith. The study of Christian origins is important for the understanding of the Gospel and hence for dealing with the present life of the Church, but I do not think that it belongs to apologetics properly so-called which, according to our definition, is the study of the human "why" of believing.

Depth-Experiences

To present my apologetical method I wish to introduce a way of distinguishing human experiences, which I have learned from Professor Donald Evans.[2] It is possible to discern among the ordinary experiences of men some that are char-

[2] Donald D. Evans, "Differences between Scientific and Religious Assertions", *Science and Religion, New Perspectives on the Dialogue* (New York, 1968), pp. 102-07.

acterized by special depth and meaning, and consequently exert considerable influence on their lives. I wish to give these experiences a special name. I define "depth-experiences" as ordinary human experiences that are memorable, the source of many decisions and tend to unify human life.

(a) *Memorable:* A depth-experience is not necessarily something extra-ordinary, something mystical or poetic, available to a few chosen people. By depth-experience I refer to occurrences present in the lives of all men. They are memorable; they can be recalled. A man might say, "When I was 18 my life was changed considerably because I met this particular person. Something happened to me. I remember this." Or a man may remember that the book he read a long time ago really did something to him. He recalls that it made a difference.

(b) *Depth-experiences are the sources of many decisions:* Because I met this person at the age of 18, my ideas about life began to change. I started to orient my life in a different direction. I stopped spending my time in the way I had been doing it. I slowly moved into another world. My tastes changed. I began to like another kind of people. Meeting this person became for me the source of many decisions.

(c) *A depth-experience unifies human life:* What does this mean? We often experience ourselves divided into many parts: our feelings and preferences pull us in different directions. Yet, we desire to be unified. We want to possess ourselves in peace to be able to give ourselves away. Depth-experiences unify our lives. Because I met this person, or read this book, or understood this truth, or saw reality in this new way, I have become more united, less driven and pulled in different directions, more in touch with my deep feelings and my true aspirations. I have come to be more myself.

As we reflect on our past we realize that we all have had depth-experiences. They were the important experiences that made us to be who we are today. Some had to do with mother and father and the family. Then as we moved away from home, there were other experiences that were memorable, that were the sources of many decisions and that unified life. These are the experiences that keep on nourishing us in our self-possession as men.

In the following pages I wish to give a brief description of various depth-experiences. I do not suggest that they make up an exhaustive list. I do not suppose that these experiences necessarily occur in every single person. There is such a variety of human sensitivity. As we look at our life, talk to other people, read the works of literature and view plays and films, we gain insight into the great variety of depth-experiences, some of which exist in the life of every man.

Religious Depth-Experiences

First, I wish to mention two experiences that are specifically "religious". They occur only among religious people. They are usually described in religious language. While they abound in the literature of the past, there are some signs that in the present culture they do not occur as often, even among believing Christians.

The religious experience of *the holy* is a depth-experience. Throughout the ages, in all religions, men have, at certain times and places, experienced a transcendent otherness in life. Set apart from ordinary life, they have encountered a powerful, mysterious presence which inspired them with awe and reverence, and attracted them more strongly than the most beautiful things they loved. In the presence of this transcendent power man felt unclean, unworthy, in need of purification. He would tremble before the transcendent other. He would fall on his knees. He would acknowledge the infinite

qualitative difference between the other and himself in a
gesture of adoration. At the same time man would be overwhelmed with love for this mysterious presence which recalled
and yet transcended all that was beautiful and good in life.
Man would be so attracted by the divine presence that he
could never totally escape its spell.

The religious literature of the world abounds in testimonies to this experience of the holy. The bible itself records
many events where individual prophets and religious leaders
or even vast assemblies of men experienced the holy in their
encounter with God. If we want to associate the name of a
modern thinker with this experience, a man whose study of
the idea of the holy has had a profound influence on modern
theology, we might mention Rudolf Otto.

Another specifically religious depth-experience is the
feeling of radical dependency on God. We might call this
experience *contingency*. A man feels his limitation: he is little,
insignificant, provisional, and hence, essentially threatened
and insecure in himself. At the same time he is profoundly
aware that he belongs to another who is vast, strong, caring,
eternally reliable. He feels that though small and insecure, he
is part of a wider unity which has meaning and in the context
of which he finds the strength to face life. This man does not
lean on himself: to do so would inspire him with fear. This
man knows himself to be totally dependent on a transcendent
being who is on his side, protects him, nourishes him and will
be with him to prepare his future, even in times when life is
painful and the vision blurred.

Religious literature of all ages gives testimony to this experience. It is amply described in the scriptures. Many psalms
celebrate this feeling of trusting dependence. Jesus spoke about
it in the parable of the lilies of the field and the birds of the
air. As we trust the divine care, we are assumed into it. If
we want to associate with this experience a great religious

thinker who has given it a special place in his theology, we might mention Friedrich Schleiermacher.

Secular Depth-Experiences

We now turn to more secular depth-experiences. *Friendship* is an experience that is memorable, the source of many decisions and the principle of unity in life. We meet a person with whom we enter into a relationship of sharing; we bear the burden together, we know and are being known, we are committed to the same goal. Friendship is usually a slow process. We gradually gain confidence in the other which enables us to reveal ourselves. We gain the courage to be open to the other, even though this makes us vulnerable. Overcoming many unspoken fears in us, we are willing to accept the self-revelation of the other. This kind of sharing nourishes us. We become more cheerful. We begin to look at life in a new way, we discover values hidden from us before, we are able to offer more to society. Through friendship we gain a new kind of self-possession. We become more reconciled with ourselves. Since we become more ourselves, we have more energy available for the mission of life.

World literature is full of descriptions of this depth-experience. Reflecting on our life, we can usually see the marvelous effects which certain people, certain friends have had on us. A careful analysis of our experience would show that friendship is more than people liking one another, more than a superficial feeling of sympathy; the depth-experience of friendship is a process by which those involved are transformed. They are brought to some self-knowledge, they gain greater freedom and become more certain of who they are.

Related to friendship, though distinct from it, is an experience that may be called *encounter*. Sometimes people meet only for an hour, or a relatively short period, a few days or a few weeks, and yet they find that through the conversation and the exchange that takes place, their lives are significantly changed. Sometimes the encounter is like the good things that may happen between a teacher and his student, between the therapist and his patient, or between a man who loves life and one who is still learning to love it. There are many kinds of encounters. Some of them are undoubtedly depth-experiences. We remember them long after they happened; they affected our lives; we make many new decisions because of them, and they allow us to possess ourselves with more confidence and peace. Here each person has his own story to tell.

If we wish to associate the name of a great religious thinker with the depth-experience of friendship and encounter, we might mention Martin Buber.

Conscience is a depth-experience. For some people the experience of moral responsibility is the great reality of their inner life, in which the depth of human existence is disclosed to them. At certain moments in their lives in particular, they come to see the radical difference between good and evil and the extraordinary significance of the choices men are called to make. The options to which we are summoned make us tremble. The orientation toward goodness, fidelity, growth, toward life itself is present deep within us; and while we also feel the vehement pull of other layers of our personality toward superficiality and destructiveness, the summons that comes from the depth makes us marvel. In the experience of conscience we realize the call to be the maker of our own future. For by choosing evil we act against what is deepest in us and initiate our own undoing, and by opting for the good, we are faithful to what is deepest in us and thus open ourselves to life.

Conscience is a depth-experience. The literature of the world, whether religious or secular, gives witness to the memorable character of this experience. Men are made by it. It becomes the source of many decisions in their lives and it unifies and elevates their personalities beyond their own expectations. Religious persons have always thought that in their conscience they are in touch with a transcendent mystery: they have always believed that the voice of conscience is the echo of God's Word. If we want to associate the name of a great Catholic thinker with this experience, a thinker who has assigned to conscience a central place in Christian theology, we might mention John Henry Newman.

Truth is a depth-experience. Questions pose themselves in our lives all the time. Some of them demand answers. Unless we know the truth, we cannot grow, be faithful to ourselves and to our mission in life. While every man desires to know the truth about himself and his world, there is also something in us that is afraid of truth. We shy away from it. We prefer our own illusions and projections. At certain moments in our lives, however, perhaps through a conversation with others, through research or reading, through listening to a voice, our resistance to truth is overcome and we open ourselves to the reality before us. We suddenly see the picture. The truth has been there all the time, but we did not want to face it: by a kind of conversion we now have been opened to it. Now we see. And because we see, we are able to plan our life differently, make decisions in a new way, and enter more deeply into personal unity. Truth is a depth-experience.

The experience of truth takes place on various levels. For some people the discovery of truth has been something specifically religious. For others it had to do with self-knowledge. Again for others, the experience had to do with the meaning of life or the structure of reality. To associate a name of a great thinker with this experience, a thinker who understood his life as a series of conversions to truth and who profoundly analyzed what is involved in man's openness to truth, we want to mention Saint Augustine.

Many other depth-experiences may be described. I wish to mention two of them, that are characteristic of our own day, though by no means exclusively contemporary. I shall call these experiences the sense of human solidarity and compassionate protest. The sense of *human solidarity* goes beyond the experience of friendship. It includes all men. It makes us aware, in an overpowering way, of the unity of the human family and its common destination to growth and reconciliation. The experience transcends our ideologies; it may even shatter them. The interconnectedness of modern life and the smallness of the earth have created conditions where the sense of human solidarity has become a common experience. We know that we belong together. We realize that we depend on one another. We share in the joys of people everywhere and we suffer from the common illness. We recognize the deathly character of prejudice, hatred, discrimination. This is a memorable experience. We may recall a particular meeting or a film, or a book, or a worship service in which this sense of human solidarity gained ground in us. For some people this experience has become the source of many decisions. In the present race conflict, the sense of human solidarity makes new demands on us and prompts us to new kinds of choices. A new sense of being in solidarity with the whole human race has a profound influence on people's personal lives. Religious people, in particular, find that this experience demands a rethinking of their inherited positions which tended to confine their love to members of their own religious institution. Human solidarity beyond religious divisions is an experience that is characteristic of the present age.

To associate the name of a great man, loved universally, with this experience, a man in whom this experience has borne astounding fruits, we shall mention Pope John.

Connected with the sense of human solidarity is the experience of *compassionate protest*. Some people are deeply disturbed by the misery in life. They are burdened by the presence of injustice, exploitation, war. They feel for those who are without hope in this world. And yet they realize that the more fortunate section of mankind, the people who sit at the top, who have access to the good things of life, are also wounded by the misery of life from which they seem to have escaped. The same illness touches them also. They, too, are trapped. Slavery damages not only the slave but also the slave owner. Seeing the world thus caught in misery, some people are moved to compassion. They do not hate anyone. They identify themselves especially with the underprivileged, the exploited, the mute. Since there seems to be nothing we can do, since injustice is so deeply rooted in the system firmly established among us, the only possible expression becomes that of protest. To avoid becoming a silent accomplice in the crimes of the world, these men speak out as prophets, as accusers, as critics, even if this should provoke the enmity of society and thus, possibly, their personal undoing. Compassionate protest has become for some people in our day the only way to discover and preserve their dignity as persons.

A man who was profoundly moved by this depth-experience, and whose life was largely formed by it, was Martin Luther King.

Depth-experiences are universal. They exist in the lives of all men. As we look back over our lives we are able to detect some of the formative events which made us who we are. There is a great variety of these experiences: some people are open to one kind, others to another. While it is difficult to generalize, it seems to me that there are many people in the present secular culture, even among Christians, who have never had a depth-experience that is specifically religious— the experience of the holy and of contingency.

Depth-Experiences Are Objective

To some readers the very word "depth-experience" may suggest a purely subjective reality. But depth-experiences as described in these pages are man's response to reality. A man's sentiment is purely subjective when it does not correspond, in proportion and quality, to the reality before him. Sentimentality is no guide to truth. For this reason men must always submit their feelings and experiences to critical reason, to test whether their responses to life are valid. This kind of testing does not invalidate the deep experiences men have: on the contrary, it establishes some of these deep experiences as authentic responses to reality, human and divine. Through his depth-experiences man is in touch with true values: they have, therefore, a certain cognitive content. These experiences bring us in touch with reality and, in this sense, are truly objective.

The Thesis of This Chapter

After this description of depth-experiences, I am able to formulate the thesis of this chapter. People become Christians and stay Christians if the Gospel of Christ explains, purifies and multiplies their depth-experiences. Before examining this thesis in detail, I will try to spell out its general meaning. The thesis affirms that the christian message explains why some experiences of people are more profound than others. Some experiences, we have seen, have a profound influence on human life. They are unforgettable; they are the source of many decisions affecting the orientation of life; they help men to greater personal integration. Why do men have such experiences? The christian message explains that these experiences are special because in them the God who has revealed himself in Christ, is present to human life. In depth-experiences God is redemptively present to the lives of men. The christian message, the thesis affirms, also purifies the depth-experiences of men. Through the message of Christ, we learn that all of human life is ambiguous. The need of redemption is universal. Even the marvelous things in human life, such as depth-experiences, are vulnerable. They retain a certain ambiguity. The christian message enables men to be critical in regard to their own deep experiences, discern in them what is for life and what is for death, and then turn away from the powers that destroy to the God of life. Finally, the thesis affirms, that the christian Gospel, as celebrated in the Church, multiplies the depth-experiences of Christians. The confrontation with Christ in the believing community, especially in worship, creates many deep experiences in the Christian: which is to say that his life becomes more memorable, less routine and more meaningful. Since depth-experiences are sources of many decisions and integrate life, the christian message by multiplying these experiences creates in men a greater sense of mission and purpose, and initiates them into a more integrated and peaceful self-possession.

We are now able to restate the thesis of this chapter: If the christian message explains, purifies and multiplies the depth-experiences of people, they become and stay believing Christians. This is the human "why" of believing. Preaching the christian message is the explicitation, in Jesus Christ, of God's redemptive involvement in the lives of men. If the message explains to people the precious things going on in their lives, if it makes known to them the ambiguity of their experiences and warns them of the illusions which might be hidden in them, and if it promises to intensify their significant experiences, then people come to look on the Gospel as the key to their life. It leads them to greater self-knowledge and self-possession. The Gospel provides for Christians a perpetual

verification of itself. It will continue to explain to them what
happens in their deep experiences. It will warn them of their
illusions, and more than that, it will multiply these experiences
and thus unify their lives. This is why people stay Christians:
there is a certain experimental verification of the christian
message in the Church. If the christian message no longer
explains to people their deep experience of reality and no
longer intensifies the things that unify and integrate human
life, people will lose interest in the Church. Christian faith
will become an abstract formula; eventually people will drift
away from the christian community altogether.

Our apologetical thesis, therefore, makes new demands
on the pastoral mission of the Church. For the sake of the
vitality and mission of the Church, it is imperative that we
proclaim the Gospel as the key for the understanding of
ordinary life—this is doctrine—and celebrate the gifts of
Christ in a way that is accessible to people and draws them
into the new life promised by Christ—this is sacramental
worship.

Depth-Experiences Explained, Purified and Multiplied by Christian Message

We must turn to a more detailed examination of our
thesis. We shall look at each of the depth-experiences mentioned above and examine whether and how the christian
message offers an explanation for them, how it purifies them,
and how it multiplies or intensifies these experiences in the
lives of men.

In regard to the two specifically religious depth-experiences of the holy and of contingency, our task is easy. The
biblical message deals explicitly with them.

The Holy: Both Old and New Testament give many

accounts of the experience of the holy. God's self-manifestation, according to the biblical story, often occurred in a special place, at a certain moment, in a marvelous manner that separated it from the ordinary experiences of life. People fell on their knees: they were filled with awe and overwhelmed with joy. There were moments when such manifestations took place even in Jesus Christ. At the transfiguration of Jesus, the disciples fell on their faces; they trembled with awe and yet were filled with happiness and the desire to remain there. The scriptures explain that this experience of the holy is a manifestation of God's presence to man.

At the same time the christian message also warns us of the ambiguity of this experience. The sinfulness of man touches all aspects of his life. Even his experience of the holy is in need of redemption. The experience of the holy could tempt men to divide reality into two distinct categories: the sacred and the profane. It could tempt people to be concerned with the separated area of the holy and neglect, or even despise, the area of ordinary human life regarded as profane. In other words, it is possible that men make use of the experience of the holy to escape from the real situation in which they live. Instead of transforming the environment to which they belong and thus undergo transformation themselves, they escape into a realm of the sacred, which they regard as more important than this life and which permits them to shrug their shoulders to the problems of the world with a good conscience. The experience of the holy offers the constant temptation to men to divide life. The experience of the holy can even threaten the unity of society. If people create their religion around this experience, they tend to divide men into those who are initiated into their worship and those who are outsiders.

In Jesus Christ the strict separation between the sacred and the profane has been overcome. The definitive and unconditional self-manifestation of God takes place not in a temple separated from ordinary life, but in Jesus Christ, the man among men, in his human words, his gestures, his entire person. In the incarnation is revealed to us that God is present to human life not simply at certain special moments, in sacred separation, but first of all and especially in the ordinary situations of life and history. The christian message, therefore, offers a critique of the experience of the holy. Worship is in need of being tested. Does worship bring us closer to life or does it provide an escape from reality? Does worship make us more conscious of the unity of man or does it create in us walls that separate us from other people? The christian message, therefore, purifies the depth-experience of the holy.

Does the christian Gospel celebrated in the Church also multiply or intensify the experiences of the holy? From christian literature we know that this has been true for a vast number of Christians. The worship of the Church and the tradition of prayer and contemplation have made the experience of the holy available to the christian people.

Contingency: The biblical message also offers an explanation of the experience of total dependence. God has linked himself to the human family in a covenant of mercy. The acknowledgment of this message in faith, according to the testimony of biblical literature, has always created a joyful sense of dependency. Man is a creature, and to become aware of his own creatureliness means to acknowledge his foundation in the living God of mercy and new life.

Does the christian message also purify this experience of dependence? Someone might suggest that such an experience is not in need of purification: it is always wholly good. It is always the work of the Spirit in man. Yet the message of Christ reveals to us that man is a sinner: the illness is universal. There is no experience which is not in perpetual need of being tested by the divine critique of the Gospel.

Even the feelings of absolute dependency on God can be a temptation for man to get away from the true God revealed in Christ.

In the present age when the area of human responsibility is constantly growing, extending to almost every aspect of his personal and social life, we have become painfully aware of a deadly passivity in us. There is something in us that shies away from the responsibility to which we are summoned and often tends to block the energies we need to transform our environment and thus undergo transformation ourselves. When we were children, mother and father protected us; they acted on our behalf; their judgment was dependable. As we grow up something in us still longs for the days of our childhood when life seemed more secure. We are tempted to invest people with authority or whole institutions with the wisdom and power which as children we saw in our parents. Because of the ambiguity of the human situation, men may even use God and their feelings of dependence on him, as an escape from growing up and assuming responsibility for their lives. No man ever totally transcends the hidden longing to remain a baby. The experience of dependence, therefore, could possibly feed in us a sinful passivity, the unwillingness to grow up, the fear to assume responsibility for our own future.

This experience is, therefore, in need of being tested by the christian message. Does this experience make us smaller, less capable of living and more afraid of reality? Or does it reassure us, give us strength to face life and to make decisions? God does not tie men to his apron strings—figuratively speaking. Man is not dependent on God in the sense that he expects God to make decisions for him. God's presence in human life as Father, Son and Spirit, frees man to assume his own responsibility for his future. In a certain sense God makes us independent of him. More correctly, the dependency on God, according to the christian message, gives us constant access to the divine source of freedom enabling us to see, to act and to be, and hence, to create our own history.

The christian message intensifies the experience of dependency on God in faith. The spiritual literature of all ages gives witness to this. Even today, when we have come to realize more than ever before the wide responsibility to which we are summoned and believe that God frees man to create his own future, we are still able to give meaning to the experience of total dependence. According to the christian message we depend totally on God's redemptive presence in our lives as the source of our faith, our courage, our creativity, our hope, our power to love. We are dependent on God who creates life out of death.

We now turn to the more secular depth-experiences. They too, we intend to show, are explained, purified, and multiplied (or intensified) by the christian message.

Friendship: The biblical message explains that friendship between people is the fruit of God's gracious presence to them. By nature, we are told, we are born into dividedness. We are born into a sinful environment where we cannot grow up without becoming a sinner. We bear the wound of self-centeredness. Part of us wants to be friends with others and part of us wants to triumph over them. The scriptural message tells us that by his will power man is totally incapable of making himself selfless. We cannot change ourselves. We cannot escape our dividedness alone. We conclude, therefore, that wherever men forget themselves and think of others, the mystery of salvation is happening to them. Grace—not will power—creates friendship. Wherever people enter into fellowship and lose a grain of their egoism, something marvelous has happened: God has been present to them. Whether they know it or not, people who through growth and reconciliation become friends, participate in the paschal mystery of Christ; the death and resurrection of Christ becomes operative in their lives. Friendship, we conclude, is a precious and formative experience because in it God is redemptively present to men.

At the same time the christian message purifies the depth-experience of friendship. Friendship must be tested by Christ. Self-seeking, ambition, destructive sensuality, or the desire for power may color the experience of friendship so that instead of promoting growth and reconciliation, it actually nourishes the destructive and hostile trends in men. Every friendship is in need of purification. Since the preaching of Christ leads to self-knowledge and conversion, and the celebration of his eucharist to a better understanding of authentic fellowship, the Gospel purifies the friendship that is present in the lives of men.

The christian Gospel multiplies and intensifies the experience of friendship. The salvation offered to us in Christ initiates us into fellowship with other Christians: grace creates friendship. In the Church we participate in a common life, bear the burden together and learn to open ourselves to other people.

Encounter: The scriptural message has also much to say about the depth-experience of encounter. We learn in the bible that God speaks to us through other men. The Word of God is not only recorded in the scriptures and proclaimed in the community, it also addresses us through people and the experience of life itself. God may speak to us through the people we meet. The biblical books tell us about many significant encounters between men, encounters which produced remarkable transformations in their lives. Sometimes a single conversation changed the entire course of a person's life. Why? Because the Word of God was present in the conversation. The briefest encounter with Jesus often meant a radical change in the lives of men. The biblical message thus explains why the encounter between persons can be a depth-experience, memorable, giving orientation and unity to life. The Word of God speaks in human conversation.

At the same time the message of salvation also warns us of the dangers that may lie hidden in the depth-experience of encounter. The demonic, too, appeals to something in us. The effect which an encounter may have on us may be destructive. It might divide us. It might make us blind to reality. It might inspire in us hatred or the desire to dominate or the pride of nation or the idolatry of race. There is the need to subject the experience of encounter to the test of the Gospel. Where does it lead? Does it make us grow in the new life which Christ has revealed?

The Gospel also multiplies the experience of encounter. Because Christians listen to God's Word proclaimed in the Church, they are sensitive to the divine summons even when speaking with other people and become open to encounters with others that have a profound effect on their lives. Through the Gospel as preached in the Church we become listeners, ready for many life-giving encounters with people.

The Gospel of Christ explains, purifies and multiplies human depth-experiences. The reader will have come to understand my method of demonstrating this assertion. I have tried to show, first, that the message of salvation presents these experiences as the gracious actions of God in the lives of men. In the above paragraphs I have simply indicated the scriptural themes: it should not be difficult to give a more detailed presentation. Secondly, I have shown that the same message of salvation demands that these experiences be tested and redeemed by Christ. This is the traditional doctrine of God's Word as judgment. Through Christ we come to the saving self-knowledge as sinners. I have tried to show, finally, that the same message of salvation, proclaimed in the Church, generates a christian life in which these depth-experiences are multiplied and intensified. The Gospel moves men ahead toward growth and reconciliation.

We must verify our thesis in regard to the depth-experiences of conscience, truth, solidarity and compassionate protest. Lest I tire the reader who has caught on to the method, I will attempt to be brief.

Conscience: It is commonly held that the Gospel explains the experience of conscience as the saving presence of God in human life. At the same time the experience of conscience is in need of being purified. We have come to realize that the primitive conscience of the child (superego), produced largely through conditioning, remains with us even after we develop a conscious conscience and are ready to direct ourselves, by our own free decisions as responses to grace, to growth and reconciliation. This primitive conscience, which remains largely unconscious, is often the source of irrational guilt feelings. For many people it becomes a tormentor. They feel guilty about things that are not sinful. They feel ill at ease when they are happy. They constantly expect some kind of punishment. They are tempted to exert their moral energies in the areas indicated by their primitive conscience rather than turn to those areas, more significant and central to personal and social life, to which a free, sensitive and enlightened conscience would lead them. The harm done by irrational guilt feelings is enormous. They never make people more holy; on the contrary, by making people look for sin where it is not, they may prevent them from discovering the true demands of conscience and the summons of God. The experience of conscience is, therefore, in need of being tested. The Gospel helps us to decide whether the voice we hear is an irrational feeling leading us to compulsive and inflexible behavior and encouraging in us infantilism and dependency, or whether the voice of conscience is the divine summons calling us to become more like Jesus, to grow in our humanity and assume wider responsibility for ourselves and our environment. Finally, it is the common christian witness that the message of salvation intensifies and multiplies the redeeming experience of conscience.

Truth: Some readers might suggest that the Gospel has little to say about the depth experience of truth. This experience at least, they might say, has nothing to do with God's redemptive presence. Yet, according to the biblical message, man is born into an inevitably sinful situation, in which he becomes alienated from himself and others. Man is divided. Part of him desires truth, yet part of him is afraid of truth. Part of him reaches out for contact with reality, yet part of him erects walls and defenses protecting him from reality. There are, of course, some truths which do not touch man deeply; to them he has no objections; they cost him very little; they simply supply him with information. But the truth that counts, the truth that changes a man's relationship to reality and hence transforms him, is both attractive and threatening. A simple example of this is self-knowledge: we have a deep desire for it, at the same time we are scared of it. We put up many defenses that prevent us from coming to know who we are. If man, divided as he is, does open himself to truth, something marvelous must have happened to him: God's redemptive presence has enabled him to leave his fear of truth behind and be open to the reality before him.

In the philosophical tradition of the West there is a strong tendency to define man by his orientation to truth. Man is open to truth; in fact his perpetual concern for truth is his principal characteristic. Man is defined in terms of his rationality. Man wants to know the truth; and hence, according to this Western tradition, the only obstacle to truth is the hiddenness of reality. Because we do not see things clearly, because reality is complex, because the object of knowledge transcends our faculty or escapes it in some other way, we find it difficult to come to the truth. In the biblical perspective, however, the obstacles to truth are also in man himself! Man is divided. It is true to say that man is orientated toward truth only if one adds immediately that he is, at the same time, afraid of it and resists it. In the biblical perspective, truth is always salvational. The situation of man's heart determines the slice of reality to which he is willing to open himself, and only as God's Word makes him a listener is he able to open himself unconditionally to reality and perceive the truth. The way to truth, according to the christian message, is always by conversion. We insist, therefore, that the christian message explains the experience of truth as the redemptive presence of God to human life.

The experience of truth, moreover, must always be tested by the Gospel. Because of the dividedness into which man is born and the fear of reality which remains in him, he is always tempted to use the experience of truth as an escape from the more important issues of his life, personal and social. Knowledge can be defense. I can use my knowledge as a screen helping me not to have to look at what is true. I can use knowledge to evade the central issues of social life and escape from the problems of personal existence. This temptation comes to every man. This is obvious among people professionally dedicated to the truth—university professors (to whom I belong). This temptation approaches all institutions dedicated to truth, including the Churches. Truth may be used as a justification for not wanting to know what is true. We insist on all kinds of truth, we affirm statements about God and the world with infallible certainty or we prove our theories with endless research and erudition; but doing all this enables us to shrug off the real issues before us. If we take a good look, we would be able to see the truth; but we are still too much afraid of it. So we use the truth which does not touch us deeply and hence hardly deserves the name of truth, to get away from the truth that might touch us deeply and transform us and the environment in which we live. For this reason then, the experience of truth must always be tested by the Gospel. Is the experience of truth an excuse for us to stay away from life? Or does truth orientate us more effectively toward the growth which is God's work in us?

Finally, the Gospel multiplies the experience of truth. The preaching of the christian message and the celebration of the liturgy summon us to conversion. In Christ we discover what in us prevents us from seeing, and in him we are enabled to open ourselves to the whole of reality and acknowledge the truth which saves.

The reflection on the biblical message proclaimed by the Church also convinces us that the depth-experiences of human solidarity and compassionate protest are the work of divine grace in men. At the same time these experiences must be submitted to the test of the Gospel; they remain in need of purification. They remain threatened respectively by the possibility of anarchical or totalitarian solidarity and by that of infantile or hate-inspired protest. I leave the amplification of this to the reader. The christian life generated by the Gospel intensifies these depth-experiences for many people; this has been true especially in our own day. We have become deeply conscious of the unity of the human race, revealed in Christ, and we have become more willing to identify ourselves with the entire world of men, especially with the exploited.

After these considerations I wish to restate the apologetical approach I have adopted. As Christians we believe that the divine reason for believing is God's powerful Word. God addresses us, through the witness of the Church or in a more hidden way, and evokes in us the response of faith. But what are the human reasons for believing? This is the apologetical question. Why does it make sense to believe? I answer that people become Christians and stay Christians if the Gospel explains, purifies and multiplies their depth-experiences. If the Gospel ceases to reveal and intensify the meaning of their lives, Christians slowly drift away from the Church and eventually cease to call themselves Christians.

Today there are many people who are not "religious". By this I mean that they have none of the depth-experiences we have described as specifically religious. If the Gospel illumines a man's important secular experiences, if it offers a critique by which to evaluate them and initiates him into a life that intensifies them, he may become a christian believer without being "religious". There are Christians who are not particularly religious. Their important experiences are not religious but secular; but since the proclamation of God's Word explains to them, purifies and intensifies the meaning of their deep secular experiences, they remain believers in the God who comes to them through these experiences. For some of the faithful, christian life has become religionless.

Depth-Questions

At this point we must reflect a little more on what depth-experiences mean in the lives of men. We have only given a partial list of them. We have not spoken at all about important experiences that may be called depth-questions. Depth-questions are experiences that are memorable, that are the sources of many decisions, and that threaten us in our personal existence. The latter characteristic distinguishes them from what we have defined as depth-experiences. Depth-questions are formative experiences. They are not restricted to a few people, people of extraordinary refinement and sensitivity; they occasionally threaten the life of every man. I am thinking here, above all, of the three depth-questions raised by sin, despair and death. Our own experience of life among people as well as the testimony of world literature tells us that the questions raised by sin, despair and death are profound, that they have had a great effect on the lives of men and that they have pushed some people into anguish and threatened the freedom and dignity of their personal existence. These three questions are able to create death in the midst of life.

Sin

How is the christian message related to these depth-questions? I wish to indicate that the christian message explains the depth-questions, purifies them, and replies to them. We begin with the question raised by sin. To be deeply troubled by sin is the work of grace in man. Because of the dividedness into which we are born, we tend to attach ourselves to superficial questions. We fret and worry about what is not very important. To discover the profound questions of life and to be deeply troubled by sin, by one's sin, by one's own participation in the sin of the world, is already God's work in us. To be troubled by deep questions liberates us from pseudo-questions. The openness to the real questions of life is already redemptive. According to biblical teaching, man by himself cannot discover his involvement in sin. It is God's Word that reveals to man that he is a sinner. It is always and everywhere an encounter with God—in some hidden way at least—that initiates man into the knowledge of his sinfulness and his need of redemption.

At the same time the christian message tells us of the possible ambiguity in the question raised by sin. A man may be deeply troubled by guilt feelings that are unreal, that do not lead him to self-knowledge and genuine repentance. We have already mentioned the primitive or childhood conscience (superego) which remains in adults, sometimes with great intensity, not as a guide to the moral life but as a tormentor making them feel guilty and thus preventing them from seeing what is morally significant. The depth-question raised by sin, therefore, must be submitted to the test of the Gospel.

Finally, the christian message replies to the depth-question raised by sin. The recognition of his share in the sinfulness of the world creates in man an anguish that threatens him in his personal existence. Life can become a valley of tears. Life can become a prison cell. Here the christian message supplies an answer: the Good News offers the forgiveness of sin. Because of Christ, because of God's self-communication to us in the life, death and resurrection of Christ, we believe that we are sons, that our sins are forgiven, that we are not caught in the traps of our own mean and stupid actions, that we are not delivered over to the forces of our own self-destructive choices, that we are forgiven, accepted, called to fellowship.

Evil

Secondly, the anxiety raised by evil is a depth-question. We may be so overwhelmed by the terrible and disastrous things that happen in life, that the world becomes a question mark to us and a source of constant pain. To be troubled and disturbed by the evil in life satisfies our definition of depth-question. This anguish threatens us in our personal existence. For as we fall into despair, we lose the energy to do, to live and to be.

According to the christian message the depth-question raised by evil is the work of divine grace. Since man is burdened with much selfishness and by himself tends to be concerned with his own affairs, to be free, sensitive, and loving enough to perceive and to suffer from the evil in human life is the work of God's liberating grace in man. People who are deeply troubled by the problem of evil are experiencing God's presence to them, freeing them from superficial attachments, opening them to what is profound, creating in them compassion.

Often people discuss with priests their doubts about the existence of a good God. They are overwhelmed by the problem of evil. An easy trust in a good deity would be, for them, a way of belittling the suffering that goes on among men. To say that God is good seems to trivialize the awful things that happen in the world. It is difficult to find a reply to such questions. What is marvelous, however, is that in this evil world there are people deeply concerned about the suffering and the misery which dominate the larger part of mankind. Because of the dividedness into which we are born, we find it easier to be preoccupied with our own little problems, our own plans, our own pleasures. The priest might well ask the questioners why this problem of evil bothers them so much while it leaves so many people cool and detached. What has happened to the man who is able to transcend his superficial concerns to be preoccupied with universal suffering? According to the christian message, God's redemptive presence has in some way touched such a man, freeing him to weep over the suffering in life. The depth-question is the work of the Spirit.

At the same time the depth-question raised by evil must be put to the test of the Gospel. It is possible in this sinful universe that a man dramatizes his concern for universal suffering to escape the particular demands which life makes on him. It is possible to give in to despair and perpetually reflect on the injustices of the world, to nourish the streak of passivity in us which prevents us from acting and living. The Gospel of Christ summons us to self-knowledge even in regard to our anxiety over the evil in the world. If our exasperation with life is inauthentic, we are in need of conversion and growth.

The Gospel attempts to reply to the depth-question raised by evil. We are told that God is not the author of evil. The scriptures may not supply us with a satisfactory metaphysical theory explaining how God is in no way an accomplice of evil, but they do proclaim the Good News that God is always and everywhere the author of life, of forgiveness, of newness, of healing, of growth, of expansion, of grace and of glory. The Good News tells us that the world is not totally lost to the powers of destruction which are present in it: something else is operating in the world, namely, the victorious mystery of redemption, revealed to us in Jesus Christ. The evil which surrounds us may in part be due to our own sinfulness; in any case, it belongs to the condition of life as we know it. The "why" of the presence of evil in human life cannot be answered. The scriptures tell us that it is not God's doing. The same scriptures tell us that God is opposed to evil, that he has conquered evil in the life, death and resurrection of Christ, and that in him men everywhere are summoned and graced to overcome evil and the powers of evil. For many people this faith lessens a little the anguishing problem raised by the presence of evil.

Death

Death, too, raises a problem that fulfills our definition of depth-question. Personal experience and the literature of all cultures convince us that death and the fear of death may stir up anxieties in men that profoundly affect their lives and threaten them in their personal existence. Why has the ineluctable reality of death been the cause of such deep questioning? The christian message suggests that death causes great anxiety because man senses that he has been destined for a future that has no end. Even if people do not explicitly believe in eternal life, they are in touch with the inner (supernatural) dynamism of their own growth and hence, whether they acknowledge it or not, with the redemptive mystery summoning them to eternal life. The fact of death is experienced by men as the great contradiction. Again, we conclude, the Gospel explains why the problem raised by death is a depth-question.

At the same time the problem raised by death must be subjected to the test of the Gospel. The Word of God, which is judgment before it is pardon and new life, helps us to discern whether the problem of death that troubles us is largely a morbid preoccupation or whether it is a genuine effect of the contradiction between earthly death and the mystery of new life that lays hold of man to make him live forever. The christian message has a special reply to the problem of death. We believe that God always creates life out of death and, therefore, that the summons toward new life present in our lives will never leave us, even as we die, but ever call us to be alive in the power of the Spirit.

These brief remarks on depth-questions complete what we have said about the human reasons for believing in the Gospel of Christ. We do not suggest that every person has had all these experiences and questions; some people may have had very few of them. But if the christian message does explain a man's depth-experiences—even if they are all of one kind—if the christian message purifies them and gives them greater meaning and scope, then he becomes and stays a christian believer.

Redemptive Involvement of God in Human Life

Before concluding this chapter we must deal with three objections. Some readers may feel that this apologetical approach makes the Good News a part of nature. They may feel that here the Gospel is simply the answer to a problem which arises in natural life and the explanation of precious experiences which are part of nature. However, the presupposition of this entire approach to apologetics is the redemptive involvement of God in human life. Life is not "natural". Human life is never simply the product of man's own resources. The divine summons, and the divine gift to respond to them, are present in the lives of all men. Man, to be sure, may close himself to the divine summons; this is true in the Church as well as outside. But whether in the Church or outside of her, human life is always and everywhere the realization of a dialogue of salvation with God. For this reason we have insisted that the depth-experience and the depth-questions are not simply "natural" events; according to the christian message, in them God is redemptively present to human life. The Good News revealed and proclaimed is, therefore, not the explanation of, and reply to, man's natural aspirations— to hold this would be a serious error—but to the aspirations which the Spirit is creating in human life everywhere. Even the profound and anguishing questions raised by sin, evil and death are due, as we have shown, to the gracious presence of God to human life. In the Gospel God replies to the questions which he, himself, poses in the hearts of men. God gives the question before he gives the answer; and as we have indicated, the question itself, if created by the Spirit in us, is already a redemptive reality—even if we do not hear the answer contained in the eternal Word made flesh in Jesus.

The Strict Obligation To Believe

A second objection which may be raised is that the apologetical approach outlined in these pages does not take seriously the strict obligation to believe. Jesus Christ repeatedly declared that either a man believes and lives, or else he refuses to believe and dies. When God's Word addresses a person, faith is not optional to him; it is demanded. Either he opens himself to the message in faith and becomes a new creature, or else he rejects the message and excludes himself from the source of life. We note that Maurice Blondel himself raised this objection against the apologetics of the 19th century. Traditional apologetics, he said, only proved that divine revelation is credible, but failed to show why it is imperative for a man who has been addressed by God, to believe. The traditional apologetics sought to demonstrate the divine origin of the message but did not attempt to show that there is something in the message itself that made faith an obligation. According to this traditional approach, as critically evaluated by Blondel, the Gospel was regarded as supplementary, optional information about God and the supernatural order. Blondel, himself, in his apologetics, tried to show that in the Spirit-created dynamics of human life there is an intrinsic demand to believe the Gospel. On this point I follow Blondel—with an important qualification.

It is the clear teaching of the scriptures that man addressed by God's saving Word is not free to reject it. The Word evokes faith in man. If a man closes himself from this and destroys the gift God is creating in him, he chooses death. There are situations in life when a man has only two choices: either he trusts the Word of God and enters into life, or he turns away from this Word and destroys himself. This harsh teaching of Jesus is as valid today as it was in his days. But when do men find themselves in this situation? When are men addressed by God's Word in such a way that unbelief is entry into death? This may happen, in some cases, when a man hears the Gospel preached for the first time. It may happen when men come in contact with the teaching of the Church. But it may also happen—and this is true for the majority of men—at various moments of their lives when the Word of God addresses them from within their situation and when the only choice available to them is to trust life or to become deaf and die. The harsh teaching of Jesus remains valid; but reflecting on the presence of the divine Word in human history, we hesitate to suggest that the summons which spells out judgment and demands faith, comes to men when they encounter the christian message in the Church. This may be true for some; others may learn through the christian message that the important decisions in their lives took place many years ago when they turned away from despair to faith in the newness God creates in them. Because God is redemptively involved in the dynamics of human life, human life does imply the obligation to believe; but we do not know the moment when this demand confronts men. Nothing in our experience suggests that this moment is usually the encounter with the Church's preaching.

For this reason, then, it seems to me that an apologetics need only show the human reasons for believing the christian message; it need not attempt to show that the Gospel preached by the Church creates in people the obligation to believe. Today we tend to think that people may have valid reasons for not accepting the christian message. If this message— because of the way and the context in which it is announced —fails to explain, purify and intensify the depth-experiences of men, they have no human reasons available to them for becoming Christians. At the same time we are more willing today to admit the reality of saving faith, created by the Spirit, implicit in man's response to God's Word present in human life.

Objective Foundations of the Faith

A third objection might insist that this apologetical approach moves in the subjective order and hence seems to belittle the objective and historical reality of the christian faith. I reply that the study of the origins of the Church, and hence of the historical foundations of the christian message, is extremely important; but it does not belong to apologetics. The historicity in general, not in detail, of the great salvational events recorded in the scriptures and testified by the people of Israel and the christian Church, is quite adequate for people who become and stay christian believers. In the New Testament we are in touch with the witness of the early Church. That there is an historical foundation, in a general sense, to the faith of the apostolic community is obvious. Few, if any, historians today want to reduce the christian story to a legend. In this general sense, the historical basis of the christian faith stands quite firm. What apologetics deals with is whether this faith makes any sense today. Why are people today willing to join the faith of the apostolic community?

To the same objection, moreover, I would reply that the depth-experiences to which we have attributed crucial importance are not "subjective" realities, in the sense that they are unfounded sentiments, devoid of cognitive content, produced by the unstable character of the emotional life. Depth-experiences are the formative experiences which create the human person. We come to be who we are through these important experiences. They are not "subjective"; on the contrary, they establish our contact with reality, they permit us to communicate with other people, the world, and God's presence, and they constitute our objective consciousness. The apologetical approach of this chapter, therefore, brings out the objective reality of the faith which makes the Church the community of believers.

III
The Church as Hermeneutical Principle

In the last chapter we dealt with the human reasons why people believe in the christian Gospel. We now turn to the apologetical question in regard to the Church. Why are Christians Catholics? Why do Catholics think that the Gospel is available to them most authentically in the Catholic Church? Obviously it is impossible to demonstrate the mystery of redemption present in the Catholic Church. From a theological viewpoint, the ultimate reason why people join and stay in the Catholic Church is the Word of God addressing them and evoking in them the faith to receive the gifts of Christ. Yet, we cannot avoid the apologetical question altogether. What is the human "why" for being a Catholic?

APOLOGETICS FOR THE CATHOLIC CHURCH

This question poses itself with great urgency today. Does the claim of the Catholic Church to be the one Church of Christ still make sense? Is this claim, endorsed in the documents of Vatican II, the last remnant of ecclesiastical pride, or does it have a meaning for the modern ecumenically-minded Catholic? For several reasons the Church's claim to unicity has become a very difficult issue in our day. What are some of these reasons?

Traditional Arguments No Longer Valid

In the first place the traditional apologetical arguments in favor of the Catholic Church's uniqueness are generally no longer regarded as valid. We cannot offer a strict historical proof that the Catholic Church is in essential continuity with the Church of the New Testament. As Catholics we affirm this continuity because we believe that the developments that took place in the Church and her ministry were guided by the Spirit who preserves the Church in the original apostolic gifts; but few historians today would suggest that this continuing self-identity of the Church can be demonstrated historically. When, for instance, we look at the profound change that occurred in the early Church when the monarchical episcopate replaced other forms of apostolic ministry, we realize that we cannot "prove" that throughout this change the Church remained identical with herself. We believe that the Church has remained the same throughout this change because this change, tested by the scriptures, was acknowledged by the entire christian community and its leaders, and this universal consensus indicates to us the presence of the Holy Spirit.

We also have lost the taste for the apologetical argument that appealed to the unity, catholicity, holiness and apostolicity of the Catholic Church. In traditional apologetics, we tried to prove that the Catholic community exhibits more unity and universality, more holiness and greater fidelity to the apostolic heritage, than do other christian Churches. The Catholic Church, we used to argue, has four marks which distinguish her from other ecclesiastical bodies and certify her as the true Church of Christ. Today we have great hesitations in proposing such an argument. We rather regard unity, catholicity, holiness and apostolicity as the promises of Christ, revealing the marvelous things he is doing in the Church.

The presence of the risen Christ in the Church brings people into a fellowship (unity) which transcends the barriers of nation and culture (catholicity): he forgives them their sins and initiates them into new life (holiness) and keeps them faithful to the original apostolic witness (apostolicity). These four marks, then, announce the mystery of redemption taking place in the Church. At the same time they accuse the Church of sin. Remembering the four marks of the Church, we discover in how many ways we are *not* united, *not* universal, *not* holy and *not* faithful to the original gift. The four marks proclaim the redemptive action of Christ and denounce the extent of our failures. They are both gifts we receive, and tasks summoning us. This twofold character of the four marks prevents the contemporary theologians from using them in an apologetical argument.

The Catholic Church, thanks to the ecumenical movement, has come to acknowledge the other christian communities as Churches. This is another reason why the Catholic claim to uniqueness has become problematic today. The conciliar documents of Vatican II admit that the other christian Churches are used by the Holy Spirit to save and sanctify men. Even if Vatican II believes these other Churches to be variously defective in the original gifts of Christ, it gladly acknowledges that Christ is present in these Churches, in their message, in their worship and in their life of faith, hope and love.[1] The continued claim of the Catholic Church to be the Church of Christ in a unique sense in no way implies that the other Churches are not means of grace; neither is

[1] "The separated Churches and ecclesiastical bodies as such, though we believe they suffer from the defects already mentioned, have been by no means deprived of significance and importance in the mystery of salvation. The Spirit of Christ has not refrained from using them as means of salvation which derive their efficacy from the very fullness of grace and truth entrusted to the Catholic Church" (*Decree on Ecumenism*, art. 3).

this claim an invitation addressed to other Christians to leave the Churches and become Catholic. As Catholics we desire for other Christians what we desire for ourselves: namely, that they become more faithful Christians and intensify their own Church's involvement in the movement for unity and renewal. The unity we seek cannot be achieved by the conversion of one group of Christians to the confessional position of another. If there is hope for christian unity, then it will have to come about through the growing together of Christians and their Churches in such a way that each Church remains faithful to what it regards as its precious, Spirit-created tradition. What does the Catholic claim to uniqueness mean in this new ecumenical vision? Would it not make more sense to abandon it?

There is a third reason why the self-understanding of the Catholic Church as the one Church of Christ has become a thorny problem for modern Catholics. The contemporary movement of renewal has produced healthy self-criticism in the Church. We have learned to look at ourselves more honestly. Instead of defending ourselves against the accusations of others and pretending that we live up to the image we have created for ourselves, we are ready to see our faults and failings and even to examine and discuss them publicly. We have become conscious of the burden which the Church's institutional life lays on many people. Institutions always create situations in which legalism, inflexibility, authoritarianism, ideology and self-justification have access to the life of society. Since the institutional structures of the Catholic Church reflec. the social ideals of another age, since for centuries the ecclesiastical government has refused to adjust to new forms of institutional life, the ills by which all institutions are threatened are particularly obvious in the Catholic Church. The ecclesiastical government, for instance, has never accepted the division of the legislative and judicial powers, which lies at the basis of modern social life. The antiquated institutional patterns create ills which the goodwill and holiness of the bishops alone cannot overcome: the institutions themselves are in need of reform.

Catholics have no difficulty in accepting the Church's collegial structure, that is, the interconnectedness of pope and bishops in the exercise of their leadership. Catholics believe that this collegial structure developed through the guidance of the Spirit on the foundations laid by Christ. What many Catholics object to, however, is the concrete institutional enbodiment of this collegial structure, which in part reflects the feudal ideals of another age. They are convinced that the Church's divinely-given structure (pope and bishops) can be adapted to suit the organizational ideals of any age, including the present one. At this time, however, many patterns and procedures of the ecclesiastical government in the Catholic Church are antiquated (v.g. the election of the pope by the cardinals, the appointment of the cardinals, the manner of appointing bishops, the absence of ecclesiastical courts, the hiddenness of many governmental procedures, the excessive centralization, the lack of participation in decision-making). These ecclesiastical processes are more antiquated than in most Churches. In this context the unique place of the Catholic Church has come to mean very little, if anything at all to many Catholics.

Catholic Meaning of the Claim to Uniqueness

What then, taking into account these difficulties, does the Catholic claim to uniqueness mean? What, in other words, are the reasons that Christians are Catholics? I have dealt with this apologetical question in a recent book entitled *The Credibility of the Church Today*. I have tried to show there, in some detail, that the Catholic Church is necessary for the true understanding of the Gospel. The Catholic Church, in other words, is an hermeneutical principle. I wish to summarize my argument in this chapter. These reflections of an apologetical nature will lead to a wider issue, crucial in the Church today and intimately related to the problems of faith, namely the re-interpretation of doctrine.

1. What characteristics in the life of the Catholic Church could give meaning to her claim to uniqueness? First, I suggest, the Catholic Church is the only Church at this time which is able to formulate a doctrinal consensus that is accepted as normative by all its members. How is such a consensus being formed? The Holy Spirit makes Christians reflect on the scriptures and sensitive to the Word present in their history, personal and social. Through the experience of the christian life the Spirit creates deep convictions in people about the meaning of the Gospel today. Yet men interpret the message of the Gospel differently. They differ in their estimation of the principal problems arising in their culture and in their discernment of the reply God's Word gives to these problems. But conversation and cooperation, a process in which again the Spirit is involved, allow Christians to learn from one another, to become critical in regard to their positions, and to be confirmed in their own convictions by the witness of a growing number of brothers. Through such a process a consensus on the meaning of the Gospel spreads in the Church. Thanks to the collegial structure (pope and bishops) there is an authoritative coordinating system for uniting the various parts of the Church in conversation, for assuring the freedom of the local Churches and yet for protecting the unity of the universal Church, and eventually for authoritatively formulating the consensus which is being produced by the Spirit in the entire community. The collegial structure, with its

built-in tension between pope and bishops, creates a social dynamism through which the whole Church remains in conversation with all of her parts and by which the deep convictions of Christians about the meaning of the Gospel can be sifted, submitted to the test of the scriptures and eventually, through a gift proper to the bishops, be expressed in a doctrinal statement that will be accepted by the Catholic community not as an imposition from above but rather as the crystallization of its deep convictions.

2. I suggest that the Catholic Church is the only Church at this time which is able to reformulate the christian Gospel as the Good News for the contemporary world. What are the reasons for this claim? First, the Catholic Church—as we have just seen—is capable of arriving at an authoritative doctrinal consensus. Secondly, the Catholic Church has always insisted that the handing on of the Gospel, once for all revealed, is a process in which the Spirit is involved. The traditioning of the Gospel is not the repetition of an ancient formula, it is not the reiteration of biblical sayings. It is a process in which the Spirit is creatively present. In a new situation, with new questions in mind and a different experience of the world, Christians assimilate the Gospel in faith, make it their own, apply it to new issues and see in it the answer to the problems facing them. This is a creative process. The Catholic Church acknowledges this process in her teaching on divine tradition. Tradition, according to Catholic theology, does not simply refer to the past. Tradition is what happens in the present. It is the living process by which Christians formulate their witness to Jesus Christ and hand on the message of salvation to others. The Catholic Church is convinced that the Word of God, addressing her now, enables her to hand on the original Gospel in a creative process—not simply repeating past doctrinal formulations but

also re-interpreting them in the light of her present experience
of the Gospel. Because of her collegiality (pope and bishops)
and her affirmation of a divine tradition, the Catholic Church
is open to the future. This is the position I have tried to
establish in *The Credibility of the Church Today*. The Church
need not be tied to past doctrinal definitions; she is able to
re-interpret her ancient teaching in the light of God's on-going
self-communication in his Word, taking place in her now.
We will have to look at this process of handing on the Gospel
in greater detail further on.

The Gospel Understood at Vatican II

Are these theoretical considerations based on the Church's
present experience? I hold that at Vatican II the Catholic
Church has experienced herself as capable of dialogue, sifting
convictions and formulating doctrinal consensus. At Vatican
II, moreover, the Catholic Church has begun to re-formulate
the christian message as the Good News for the present age.

At Vatican II the focus of the Gospel has changed or, more
modestly, has begun to change. Instead of focusing on what
God in Christ is doing in the Church and in the individual
Christian, the conciliar documents, in several significant
places, focused on the marvelous works of God in Christ
taking place in the whole human race. Who are we? Who
are other people? Do we have a destiny? These questions,
expressing the concern of our age, preoccupied Vatican II.
Good News tells us that God in Christ is redemptively involved
in the lives of all men. Good News tells us that wherever
people are, they are not simply caught in sin, in destructive
game playing: something else is going on in their lives, summoning them to growth and reconciliation. This something
is not of their own making nor reducible to human resources.

It is the transcendent mystery of redemption. In Jesus is made known to us that this mystery appealing to people, wherever they may be, is the self-communication of God as Father, Word and Spirit. In Jesus Christ and him alone is disclosed the mystery that takes place everywhere. In him we learn who we are, who people are. In him the human is disclosed to us.

This, I propose, is the new focus of the Gospel, in the light of which the teaching of the Church must be re-interpreted. Does Vatican II actually teach that God is redemptively involved in human life everywhere? This position is not consistently proposed. The conciliar texts, we recall, are not unified documents. They are the work of committees, and hence represent various tendencies and schools of thought. What I claim, and have established in several studies, is that the redemptive understanding of the human life had so widely spread among Catholic theologians, beginning with Blondel at the end of the last century, that it was able to exert considerable influence at the Council and determine the composition of several important conciliar texts. In particular the *Constitution on the Church in the Modern World* was almost wholly written in this new perspective.[2] In this document we find the specific statement that the death and resurrection of Christ is present and available in the whole of humanity. Because of Jesus Christ, the document says, we must hold that God in a hidden manner offers to every man a share in the paschal mystery.[3] The world of men is not only the place of sin: it is also the place where an even stronger power is at work, a power which transcends man, a power of redemption initiating people into new life, into fellowship, into the true meaning of their humanity. This power is God's gift of himself to men. This divine self-communication has become

---

[2] See G. Baum's commentary in *Const. on the Church in the Modern World*, Paulist Press, New York, 1967, pp. 1-35.

[3] *Const. on the Church in the Modern World*, art. 22.

visible, definitively and unconditionally, in the man Jesus Christ.

This new focus of the Gospel is not found in all the conciliar documents. It is my view, however, that the meaning and impact of Vatican II cannot be grasped by a simple reading of the official documents. These documents contain many themes, old and new, and do not attempt to synthesize the older positions with the new insights. To estimate the significance of the conciliar documents it is necessary to study the doctrinal evolution that took place at the Council itself. We must study the first draft put on the Council floor, then the discussion that followed, then the new draft, the episcopal speeches and recommendations, the amended draft, the final modifications and, finally, the definitive version. Such a study reveals the evolution that took place at the Council. It brings out the new ideas that entered the conciliar teaching, even if these were not adopted with perfect consistency to modify the entire teaching of the Council. A simple reading of the final documents, without adverting to the development that took place, does not reveal the remarkable doctrinal shift that took place at Vatican II. But we are justified, and in fact obliged, to interpret the conciliar teaching in the light of the new ideas brought up in the conciliar debate that were after some conflict, adopted in the official documents. These new positions could be made less startling by qualifying them with the traditional teaching, but such a method of interpretation would not explain why there had been an intense conflict at the Council. When the amended documents were on the Council floor, many cardinals of the Roman curia and the bishops of the minority, opposed them because, they said, they introduced new ideas, irreconcilable with traditional Catholic teaching. After these documents were acknowledged by the Council, these same voices tried to weaken the meaning of the texts by insisting that they said nothing that the Church had not always taught. But if the texts said nothing new, why did these men oppose them so vehemently in the first place? The bishops of the minority understood very well that the new positions introduced principles into the Church's teaching that would eventually modify her entire doctrinal system. We are justified, then, in stressing the new teachings of Vatican II that attempt to deal with the problems of the Church in the present age. While we admit that these positions are accompanied by texts that reflect an older theological orientation, we understand Vatican II as the Church's answer to the questions of the present age and hence give preference to those doctrinal themes that deal with these contemporary issues. Vatican II has shifted—or at least begun to shift—the focus of the Gospel to make it the Good News for the world of today. The Good News tells us that God is redemptively present to human life.

The Catholic Church, we suggested, is Church in a unique sense. Thanks to her collegial structure (pope and bishops) she is able to come to an authoritative doctrinal consensus and, thanks to her understanding of divine tradition, she can reformulate her teaching of the past as the Good News for the present. This was the experience of the Catholic Church at Vatican II. This elucidation of the Catholic claim to uniqueness summarizes my apologetical approach in regard to the Church.

RE-INTERPRETATION OF DOCTRINE

The Church, we said, is able to reformulate her witness to divine revelation. Something like this happened at Vatican II. The focal point of the Gospel was shifted so as to reply to the contemporary threats to human existence. We must study this process more carefully. Here again I shall follow and expand the line of thought developed in my book *The Credibility of the Church Today*.

Development of Doctrine

A development of doctrine in the Church is universally recognized today. It was acknowledged explicitly by Vatican Council II. Usually this development is understood as the reflection of the Church on her inherited doctrine, giving rise to a passage, guided by the Spirit, from what is implicitly contained in this doctrine to an explicit formulation. Reflection on doctrine, tested by scripture and christian experience, brings out the hidden implications of traditional teaching. In particular, as the Church reflects on her own tradition in the light of the new problems facing her, she may be able to derive the answers to these problems from the doctrines she has always held. This passage from what is implicit in doctrine to an explicit formulation is usually called homogeneous development.

Today many theologians insist that homogeneous development is not the only kind of doctrinal development. What takes place when the Church enters a new culture or a new age is a non-homogeneous doctrinal development. For instance, more took place in the passage of the Gospel from a Jewish environment to the Hellenistic world than the reflection on doctrine and the clarification of hidden implications. What took place was a shift to a new idiom. When the Church lives in a new setting, defined by problems of a new kind and by a different language, she learns to declare the Gospel as the message of salvation for the people of her day. How can she do this? Can she simply translate the received doctrine into a new vocabulary? The answer is no. The first thing that takes place is that Christians come to belong to the new cultural setting and there experience the Gospel in a new way. Listening to God's Word as men of a different culture, they will eventually formulate their christian faith in a new way. They will experience in a new way the threats to human life, implicit in their culture, and discover in faith that the Gospel addresses itself to these threats to offer salvation from them. We have insisted in our first chapter that faith is not new knowledge: it is rather the initiation into new consciousness. The Word of God creates a new self-consciousness in the Church. The Word of God initiates us into a new way of experiencing ourselves and of relating ourselves to our environment. It is this process, evoked by the on-going self-disclosure of God in the Church, which produces a reformulation of doctrine. This development is not simply the passage from the implicit to the explicit: it represents, rather, a certain doctrinal shift. As the Church enters a new culture the doctrinal development that takes place is an original, Spirit-created formulation—tested again and again by the apostolic witness—of the self-identical Gospel spoken by God in the Church.

First Step in Re-Formulating Doctrine

We want to analyze this process more carefully. The *first step* in reformulating the Church's doctrinal witness in a new culture, is the search for the question. In every age the demonic takes on different forms. In every age human existence is threatened in different ways. The first inquiry of the Church in a new cultural age is to find the deepest questionings of men. How are we being threatened in our humanity? What are the demonic possibilities of our culture? What are the destructive powers implicit in our lives? The discernment of the basic question is already the work of the Spirit.

The sinfulness of man always tempts him to focus on superficial questions so as to evade the profound ones. Man tends
to be concerned about what is peripheral so as to avoid facing
the crucial problems raised by reality. The discernment of
the true question is, therefore, already the action of God's
Word in man. The Church, in whom this Word is alive, is
capable of discerning the central questionings of men in the
new age.

At Vatican II the bishops dealt with the self-questionings
of men in the present age. In the *Constitution on the Church
in the Modern World,* the Council clearly acknowledged that
mankind is entering a new cultural age.[4] In the strongest terms,
the conciliar text speaks of the social, intellectual, moral and
religious transformations that are taking place. It describes
"the broad and deep revolution" that is occurring in humanity
at this time. The conciliar text outlines the cultural transformation that is taking place in order to grasp man's deepest
questioning in this new situation. How are we threatened today
in our human existence, personal and social? We are told that
the crucial problem today is man's own self-questioning. Who
is man? Who are we? Who are we as persons and as community? Where are we going? What is the meaning of life
and of history?

It is not difficult to elucidate the basic questioning, characteristic of the present age. We shall limit ourselves to a
few remarks. Today we are attacked in our self-identity. When
we lived in a more static world, with stable institutions and
norms of life acknowledged by the whole of society, we were
able to define ourselves. We knew who we were. We could
express our identity in terms of the family, the nation, the
culture and the Church to which we belonged. The stability
of our environment served as matrix of our self-understanding.
The fixed framework of our life gave us self-assurance. Today

[4] *Ibid,* art. 4-10.

we have come to live in a more dynamic environment. Institutions are being transformed, sometimes even violently, and the values we live by are being questioned, re-interpreted and even rejected. The conflict of ideas and the social tensions profoundly affect our family, our nation, our culture and our Church so that we can no longer identify with them in an unqualified manner. Our environment has become so dynamic and, sometimes, so questionable that it no longer supplies us with our self-identity. The institutions to which we belong are changing so rapidly that we can no longer define who we are in terms of them. Who are we? This lack of self-identity pervades our culture with devastating effects on the lives of men.

Who are we as community? This question, too, has become a question threatening our human existence. In the present age we have come to be a single people on a small earth, we are in touch with one another, we are affected by what is going on in every part of the world; at the same time the divisive forces have become stronger, they pit man against man, race against race, perpetuate prejudice, exploitation, injustice, violence. The possibility of self-destruction has come upon us. Who are we as a people? What is our destiny? Are we moving toward the destruction of the earth as a place where men can live, or are growth and reconciliation available to us? This question, with its personal and political implications, threatens us every day. If we do not answer it, or answer it wrongly, we may destroy ourselves in inner confusion and violent conflict.

Second Step in Re-Formulating Doctrine

After the discernment of the question comes the *second step* in the re-formulation of doctrine. The Church listens to

God's Word to find the answer to the crucial question of the age. The Church believes that the Gospel is God's saving reply to the deepest threats to human existence. Divine revelation creates a saved humanity. With the new question in mind, therefore, Christians turn to the Word of God to hear the message of salvation. First they re-read the scriptures and the ecclesiastical tradition of the past. In this process may come to light some themes, contained in these sources of faith, that have a bearing on the present problem. These themes may not have been central, they may hardly have been noticed before, but upon reading the scriptures and the Church's tradition with the new question in mind, they emerge as hints and suggestions of what salvation may mean in the present new situation.

But this is not all. The Word of God is present not only in scripture and the Church's past witness; it also speaks in the experience of Christians today and, in fact, in the contemporary experience of all men. History is the locus of the divine Word. In the expression "the signs of the times" Vatican II has acknowledged the presence of God's Word in history.[5]

Divine self-revelation is complete with Jesus Christ. In Christ God has made himself known in the definitive and unconditional way. Nothing can be added. The apostolic witness to Christ needs no supplement. Christ is the Word of God. At the same time, divine revelation is a continuing reality in the Church in the sense that God continues to disclose himself to men as Father, Word and Spirit in the identical gift of himself. What God has said in Christ, he continues to say to the Church. This Word of God, addressing Christians today, creates divine faith in them and in this way constitutes the Church as the community of believers. More than that, this on-going divine self-communication is not confined to the Church in which it is proclaimed, acknowledged and cele-

---

[5] Cf. M. Vanhengel/J. Peters, "Signs of the Times", *Concilium,* (Glen Rock, N. J.: Paulist Press, 1967), Vol. 25, pp. 143-52.

brated; it is offered to men, wherever they are, and orientates them away from their sin toward human growth and reconciliation. The Word summons all men to the new consciousness as being appointed to a destiny, listeners to the new and alive with a principle that transcends them. For this reason there are many human experiences in the Church as well as beyond her that are not simply the expression of man's own limited resources but are, properly speaking, man's encounter with the divine Word addressing him in his life. To listen to God's Word then, the Church must turn to the scriptures and her past tradition as well as to the present experience of humanity. God speaks to us through the world. God addresses the Church in his self-identical Word through the wisdom and the holiness present in the human race.

As the Church listens to the world she hears a chorus of many voices. How can she discern in this chorus the divine Word? This is a crucial question. Christians detect the divine Word present in the world by its harmony and coherence with the identical Word recorded in the scriptures and celebrated in the Church. The connaturality with Jesus Christ, which scripture and liturgy create in Christians, enables them to hear the Word of God addressed to them in human experience. The discernment of God's Word in history takes place in faith. Admittedly Christians react to the world in different ways: some hear God's Word in one aspect of modern life and some in another. But dialogue among Christians, common involvement in the issues of their age, and even the conflict in the community are ways that purify the experience of the Church, test this experience by the scriptures and produce an ever widening agreement leading eventually, through the hierarchical ministry, to a doctrinal consensus. This is the process that takes place when the Church, with the new central question in mind, listens to God's Word present in the experience of her age. By re-reading scripture and creeds, and, above all, by listening to the world of men and discerning God's voice in it, the Church is able to express the divine reply, revealed in Christ, to the crucial question. Through this process, in which the Spirit is creatively involved, the Church re-focuses the Gospel as the Good News for its own age. Because of God's presence in her life, the Church is able to find the central message and thrust of divine revelation which makes it the salvational reply to the present question that threatens to undo human life.

This second step in the reformulation of doctrine also took place at Vatican II. Re-reading the scripture and ecclesiastical tradition, the Council fathers became aware of ancient doctrinal themes on God's saving presence to all men. The *Constitution on the Church* refers to these in several places. The biblical theme that God never leaves himself without a witness and that he cares for men wherever they are, and the patristic theme of the universal Church, the Church from Abel on to the last of the elect, became part of the conciliar document.[6]

The Council also listened to the world. This is recorded especially in the *Constitution on the Church in the Modern World*.[7] What is God saying in the experience of mankind? How does he summon men from death to new life? What do the new and almost universal experiences of brotherhood and solidarity mean? They seem to burst forth among men in every society and every group, especially among those who are greatly concerned with the deep things of life. Is this new experience of universal brotherhood something demonic that enables men to seek friendship in order to avoid the Word of God and be confirmed in their sin? Or is this experience a supernatural reality, a response to a divine summons, a transformation of men through the Holy Spirit? Christians

[6] Cf. art. 2, 16.
[7] See note 2 above.

must test this new experience of universal brotherhood and solidarity with the Spirit of Jesus Christ as they know him from the scriptures. Admittedly, universal brotherhood is not a central biblical teaching! According to the New Testament, men become brothers through Jesus in the Church. According to the central line of thought in the bible, outsiders to the covenant are not brothers: brotherhood does not extend beyond the covenant. Yet, leaving the letter of scripture behind, Christians must ask if the new experience of universal brotherhood is in harmony with the spirit of scripture.

Is this experience in harmony with the Spirit of Christ? Here Christians have given diverse replies. Some have taken a negative view. Some have felt that the new experience of brotherhood implies indifferentism to truth and hence bears grave danger to the christian faith. Other Christians have insisted that this new experience is in keeping with God's universal design as revealed in Christ and an authentic expression of what the following of Christ means to the present generation. They are willing to recognize in this experience God's Word addressing the Church. They admit that there is no strict demonstration that this experience is in harmony with the biblical faith: they rely on the validity of christian experience tested by the scriptures. This latter position spread in the Church. It was formally acknowledged by Vatican II. God speaks to the Church, self-identically with his revelation in Christ, through the contemporary experience of universal brotherhood and solidarity.

Thanks to this faithful listening, the Vatican Council has been able to re-focus the Gospel. Good News is the divine reply in Jesus Christ to the crucial contemporary question of who we are as persons and as community. Good News tells us that man is not simply handed over to the destructive forces existing in him and his society: another power is present in his life, calling and gracing him to become himself in growth and reconciliation, a power that transcends him, a transforming power which is God's gift of himself. Who is man, then? The Good News declares that man cannot be defined simply in terms of his own inner resources. Man is always more than man. Man comes to be himself as person and as community through a process in which God is redemptively involved. God's self-revelation affects our personal existence: through faith we become men with a destiny, listeners to the new, alive with a principle that transcends us. God's self-revelation constitutes our destiny as people: in Jesus Christ God has adopted the whole human race. Despite the devastating powers of hatred and division, we believe that the divine mystery is present where people are, summoning men into community and transforming them as they grow in fellowship. God's self-disclosure as Father, Son and Spirit creates the destiny of the entire human family. This has become visible in the life, death and resurrection of Christ. The central message or focus of the Gospel in the present age is that God is redemptively present to man's making of man. (This message, we suggested in chapter one, can even be expressed in ordinary, non-religious, secular language.)

Third Step in Re-Formulating Doctrine

This takes us to the *third step* of the Church's reformulation of christian teaching. After re-focusing the Gospel, it is necessary to re-interpret the entire doctrine of the Church in the light of the new focus.

The focus of the Gospel, we said, is its central thrust and message, about which the entire teaching of the Church is grouped and in relation to which it acquires its full meaning. The single doctrines are oriented toward this focus and must be understood in the light of it. The doctrines of the Church are not a set of unrelated propositions; they are closely inter-related and give witness to a single reality, namely, the Word of God. In the traditional language of Scholastic theology this was expressed in the phrase, "the object *(objectum quod)* of faith is one". All the doctrines of the Church are intercon-nected through a unifying principle. For this reason, then, the re-focusing of the Gospel affects the entire teaching of the Church. The single doctrines which acquired meaning from their relationship to the previous focus must be re-interpreted in the light of the new focus so that they again constitute a unified message and communicate a single divine reality, namely, God's saving Word.

The re-interpretation of christian teaching is a gradual process. I believe that the present doctrinal uncertainties in the Church are the inevitable accompaniment of this process. Doctrines which had meaning and power at one time, in re-lation to the previous focus, now seem to hang in the air. The focus which gave them salvational meaning has been shifted; what is now demanded is that these doctrines be related to the new focus and understood in terms of it. While this process of re-interpretation is not complete, it seems impossible to assign a clear meaning to some of these doctrines. This is the reason for the doctrinal uncertainty of the present.

We have mentioned above that the doubts of Christians whether a particular doctrine is true are today usually preceded by the more fundamental question of what this doctrine means. We can resolve the doubt about the truth of a doctrine only after we know what it wants to say. In this area we have at present many unsolved questions. As Catholics we accept the traditional teaching of the Church. We believe that the doc-trinal witness of the Church has been guided by the Spirit and that the Church's past tradition on the meaning of the bible is a source of truth for us. But the question which we often are unable to answer is what these doctrines mean.

The principal effort of contemporary theologians is the interpretation of doctrine in the light of the new focus of the Gospel. This endeavor was begun prior to Vatican II. Since the Council it constitutes the principal effort of christian theology. Yet there are different theological schools and often divergent attempts to clarify the meaning of traditional teaching. Much dialogue and common research are still necessary. While Catholics accept the creeds of the Church without difficulty, they will have to learn to live with some question marks as to their salvational meaning today.

Let us be more concrete. Re-interpreting doctrines in the light of the new focus today means to relate these doctrines to the message that in Christ God has revealed his redemptive involvement in human life. The doctrines of the Church, therefore, make known to us not only the wonderful things God works in the christian community but the wonderful things he performs in the entire human family. The doctrines of the Church become for us the key for the understanding of human life and history; they make known to us the destructive powers at work in human society and the redemptive presence of God to the community of man. This sort of re-interpretation we have already undertaken in regard to the doctrine of the Word. We have said that the Word of God, which sounded in Israel and became man in Jesus Christ, is present in the lives of all men: wherever people are, we have said, they are summoned to new life. Thanks to the presence of God's Word to men, human life is always and everywhere what the Scholastics called "supernatural". Human life is always the realization of a salvational dialogue with God. This is an affirmation of the ancient teaching that the divine *Logos,* who became man in Christ, enlightens all men who come into this world and leads those who are willing to be led, to wisdom and salvation.

The doctrine of Church, understood in the light of the new

focus, tells us more than what happens in the christian community; it tells us what happens in the human community. Wherever people come together to solve their problems, enter into conversation and open themselves to one another and to their neighbors, the Holy Spirit is present, aiding them to avoid the traps into which they are tempted to fall and initiating them into new insight and fellowship. Despite the sin into which men are born and which makes them play terrible games with each other, there is a voice, a summons, a guiding light, available to those who enter into dialogue and listen to what is being said in the community. I have examined this re-interpretation of the doctrine of the Church in my book *The Credibility of the Church Today*. The Church is a message of hope for all men. For the mystery of redemption, which is professed, believed and celebrated in the Church, is at work in the entire human race. In other words, the self-communication of God, which has become concrete and visible in the man Jesus, to whom the Church gives witness by her faith, orientates the whole of human history toward growth and reconciliation. God's free gift of himself works the humanization of man. We insist that this does not make the christian Church superfluous: for in the teaching, life, death and resurrection of Jesus Christ, which the Church proclaims, the divine self-disclosure enters into the consciousness of man and thus significantly transforms human life and the orientation of history. We are able to affirm the universality of grace in the sinful world as well as the newness of life brought by Jesus Christ.

The sacraments, too, must be understood in the light of the new focus. They tell us not only the wonderful things Christ does in the christian liturgy; they also make known to us how God offers transformation to men in the ordinary situations of life. The eucharistic doctrine tells us not only that Christ comes to us through the liturgy and, through the gift of himself, transforms us into a fellowship. Eucharist also means that every meal is intended to be a means of grace. Every meal is meant to bring people closer together, reveal to them their need of help and their interdependence, enable them to overcome hostility and strengthen the bonds of friendship. If a man has not learned to eat with others and be open to the transformation offered him, nothing will happen to him when he shares in the eucharist; for in this sacramental rite Jesus Christ comes to him through the human gesture of speaking and eating in company with others. The mode of Christ's sovereign coming is that of human life. The entire sacramental life of the Church, therefore, makes known to us the hidden involvement of God in the life of man. This does not take away any of the sanctifying power of the liturgy; but instead of separating us from other people, people outside the Church, the sacraments unite us more closely with them. The liturgy makes us more sensitive to God's saving presence in life. In the Church's sacramental gestures we learn how God transforms us and others into his people.

The Gospel is the Good News about God's presence in human life. This new focus affects our understanding of Jesus Christ. Karl Rahner has re-interpreted traditional christology in the light of the new focus.[8] Every man comes to be himself through a dialogue with the divine Word. Every man is constituted as a person through his own history, in which God's gracious self-disclosure has a part. Every man is more than himself. Every man, in other words, comes to be himself through some union with the divine Word. Since men are sinners, their dialogue with God's Word is not wholly one of faith, hope and love: it includes fears and rejections, hesitations and half-hearted replies. It is the divine mercy alone which assures the continuity of this saving conversation. Despite human resistance, therefore, a man becomes

[8] See K. Rahner's essays on christology in volumes 1, 4 and 5 of his *Theological Investigations* (Baltimore, Md.: Helicon).

man precisely through his union with the divine Word. The closer this union, the more human he is. This understanding of man enables us to regard Jesus Christ as a very special case of man's universal condition. Jesus is similar to other men not simply in virtue of his human nature; he is similar to them precisely inasmuch as he is the incarnate Word. Jesus resembles other men because he, too, has come to be himself through a union with the divine Word. He is, of course, different from other men inasmuch as in him this union is an absolute one. In Jesus the union with the divine Word is what the ancients called "hypostatic": this means that the union with the divine Word constitutes Christ as the perfect man. But God's self-disclosure in his Word, personally present in Jesus Christ, is present in some way in all men. Jesus Christ, thus, reveals to us who man is and is to be. In him God discloses man unto himself. Jesus Christ is the key for the understanding of human existence.

The doctrine of Christ understood in the light of the new focus removes some difficulties for the christian believer. For if—following an ancient tradition—we regard man as a substance and God as a substance, then it is inconceivable how these two distinct substances can be united in the one man Jesus. In the more traditional theology, Jesus resembled other men simply because of his human nature: his union with God made him wholly unlike other men. If, however, we do not regard man as a substance but as a dynamic, open-ended, historical reality, who comes to be through a dialogue in which other people and ultimately the divine Word are involved, then the union of the human and the divine in Jesus appears as a special case of being human. In Jesus, whose response was not tainted by sin but determined by total openness, the divine Word communicated himself unconditionally, definitively and exhaustively. To other men God unites himself in the salvational dialogue only on condition, only as a stage, only in a limited way. But in Christ this union was absolute. He is the Word made man. Seen in this perspective Jesus Christ is the complete and perfect man precisely because he is the divine Word.

What does the new focus of the Gospel mean for the mission of the Church? Is this mission invalidated? If salvation is offered to people everywhere, is there any reason for continuing the proclamation of the Gospel in the world? Some Christians have been so deeply impressed by the omnipresence of the redeeming God to human history that they interpret the Church's mission simply in terms of service to the world. The mission of the Church, they say, is to seek identification with the whole human race, to bear the burden with the other people, to help wherever help is required, to cooperate with other men in the transformation of the human environment. As Jesus was servant, so the Church must become a servant in society. These Christians wish to define the Church's mission without reference to the message of Christ. For them christian mission is action rather than truth.

I do not follow this interpretation. The Church's mission must be defined in terms of proclamation. But what is the Church's message to the world, understood in the light of the new focus? The Church is destined to engage in dialogue with other people, with their religions and ideologies: in this dialogue the Gospel is sounded. In this dialogue the Church listens to the convictions of others and expresses her own faith in Jesus Christ in terms accessible to her partners. What is the purpose of this dialogue? Is it to convert others to the christian Church or is it an intellectual effort to supply better information to the participants? It is neither the one nor the other. Dialogue in which the Gospel is sounded is a truly redemptive ministry, thanks to which both partners enter more deeply into what is God's will for them.

Dialogue is mission. Dialogue is a way of proclamation.

Since the message of Christ reveals the ambiguity of life, since Gospel is judgment or critique, the dialogue of the Church may enable her partners to become more aware of the ambiguity of their own situation. They may learn to distinguish in their own religious or ideological systems that which is for life and that which is toward death; and by remaining in the conversation learn to attach themselves more to what is saving in their tradition and to resist the destructive elements. Through this dialogue members of other religions may become more sensitive to the elements of their tradition through which God summons them to salvation and abandon those elements which are obstacles to the humanization of man, in which God is present to history. Dialogue, in other words, is a truly spiritual redemptive process, in which the Church's partners enter more deeply into what is God's will for them. At certain exceptional moments, this dialogue might lead to their conversion to the christian faith; more generally, however, it will help other people to enter into a deeper dimension of salvation, as it is available to them where they are.

What is the effect of this dialogue on the Church herself? The Church, too, enters more deeply into what is God's will for her. Listening to others in the light of the Gospel, the Church will be able to detect the presence of God's Word in the convictions and aspirations of other people. Since God's Word is present to the Church not only in scripture and tradition but also in present history, the Church that seeks to submit herself totally to the Word of God is in need of dialogue with the whole world. The Church needs the world to become truly Church. It is easy to give examples of how Christians have learned the implications of the Gospel through dialogue with others. For instance, it was dialogue with the secular world that has taught the Church to cherish as christian values religious liberty, impartial study of texts, historical self-criticism, the generous appreciation of thinkers with whom one disagrees, etc. The Church is in need of dialogue with the world to find the true dimensions of her obedience to Christ.

In the light of the new focus, then, the urgency of the Church's mission remains. Mission is the faithful dialogue of the Church with other religions and ideologies as a means of offering redemptive transformation to all the participants, the Church as well as the others.

I have given several examples of the re-interpretation of doctrine. The entire christian teaching, especially the doctrine of God, must be re-interpreted in terms of the new focus. I hope to do this in another book. One of the great needs of the Church is to learn to speak about God and his transcendence in harmony with the contemporary experience of reality. This can be achieved, I think, through such a re-interpretation.

The re-interpretation of the Church's teaching in the light of the new focus, which is taking place in christian theology at this time, is the final step in the process we have called the reformulation of doctrine. When the Church enters a new cultural age, a doctrinal development takes place that is not simply the derivation of new insights from traditional teaching, not simply a passage from the implicit to the explicit. What occurs is a doctrinal shift. Re-focusing the Gospel as the Good News for the new age and re-interpreting the Church's teaching in the light of it, produces a reformulation of doctrine, in fidelity to the apostolic witness, that deals with the relevant issues of the present and uses concepts and language drawn from contemporary culture. Because this process began with the discernment of the burning question, the re-focused proclamation of the Good News will deal with issues significant for all men belonging to the present age. It will be easy to enter into dialogue with men of other religions and men of no religion. Living in the same cultural age, we are tormented by the same basic questions and threatened by the

same forces undermining human life. As the Church reformu-
lates her doctrine it will appear that God's self-revelation in
Jesus Christ deals with contemporary issues and offers hope
for men of today.

We repeat our contention. The Catholic Church is necessary for the understanding of the Gospel. Without the Church
we have two choices: either simply to repeat the doctrinal
formulas of scripture and tradition or to follow the interpretation based on personal experience. I contend that we need
the brothers, the whole community, to understand the meaning of the Gospel today. We need the experience of all Christians, we need dialogue in the community, common effort,
even some conflict. As a Catholic I add that we need the
authoritative ministry of the Word (bishops and pope) who
sift the convictions of the christian people and testing them
with the Gospel, come to formulate the Spirit-created consensus regarding the central thrust and message of the Gospel.
Thanks to the living Church, the apostolic witness, once for
all delivered to the saints, can become for every age the Good
News saving men from the enemies of life and initiating them
into their redemptive destiny. In short, the Church is a necessary hermeneutical principle for understanding divine revelation.

CATHOLIC HERMENEUTICS

The hermeneutical question is central in the christian
Church today. What is the meaning of scriptural message and
ecclesiastical doctrine? What principles do we use in order
to grasp the truth that christian teaching intends to communicate? How can we faithfully proclaim the Gospel once for all
revealed? How can we guard the faith of the ancients?

The problem is difficult. A simple reflection convinces us

that we cannot say what the ancients said by repeating the same words; to communicate the same reality, we have to say something different. If we do repeat their words and expressions, we are in fact saying something quite different— except, perhaps, to a small group of people who choose to live apart from the present age and retain the cultural mood of antiquity. We cannot be faithful to the message revealed in Christ simply by reiterating the scriptural witness or the creeds of antiquity. In the first place the meaning of words has changed; we no longer associate the same reality with them. When the ancient words are sounded, we do not hear what the ancients heard. Secondly, and this is even more important, the biblical message refers to God's covenant with men in Jesus Christ, and therefore has to do with a living, historical community. The biblical message reveals God's relationship to his people. But since this covenanted relationship has a history since the days of the apostles, we cannot proclaim this relationship simply by repeating the words that expressed it in the past. Because this relationship has grown, because God has replied to man's questions and healed man's wounds in many new situations in history, the witness to God's self-communication today must reflect this historical experience. The self-identity of the Gospel message is not preserved by repeating the ancient formulas: to announce the selfsame Good News today we have to use a new formulation. If we do restrict ourselves to saying the same thing, then we actually falsify the message—at least for the vast majority of our contemporaries.

That the Church cannot be faithful to the Gospel by repeating the original message but that, in order to preserve it, she may have to reformulate and, hence, change it, is acknowledged in the Catholic doctrine of "divine tradition". The ecumenical councils of the 4th and 5th centuries gave faithful witness to the Gospel of Christ, but in keeping with the language and the questions of the age, they expressed this witness in non-scriptural terms and in a non-scriptural perspective. These councils defined aspects of the divine message with which the scriptures were not especially concerned. But to proclaim and protect divine revelation in the Church of those days it was necessary to modify the doctrinal formulation. The self-identity of the living Gospel in history is assured only through a development of doctrine.

We note that the self-identity of a non-living thing is preserved if it does not change. If you visit your home after an absence of ten years, you may find in the backyard the same, large rock lying near the fence. "The same rock," you exclaim, "the identical rock I knew when I was a child: it has not changed at all." The self-identity of the rock manifests itself in its immutability. The self-identity of a living thing, however, is preserved only if it changes. Imagine that visiting your home after an absence of ten years, you meet again the boy who lives next door. When you had left, he was five years old, a bright and lively child. Imagine that he had not changed in the years of your absence. Seeing him again on your return, you would exclaim, "What happened to you? You have changed. You used to be a normal child, and now you are retarded." The self-identity of a living being is preserved only if it changes, grows, develops, expands. If a living thing does not change, it changes. In order to preserve its self-identity a living thing must constantly regain and repossess itself, reassimilate its changing environment and respond in ever new ways to the community to which it belongs.

The Gospel is a living reality. It is the self-communication of God in Christ, proclaimed by the Church. To preserve the self-identity of this proclamation, the Church must reformulate her doctrinal witness as she moves from age to age. We cannot protect the Gospel by repeating the ancient formulas. If we insist on repeating them without qualification, we may actually announce another message and hence fail to mediate the divine self-communication to men.

These reflections point to the extraordinary importance of the hermeneutical question in the contemporary Church. If it is true that we have entered a new cultural age, how can we protect the self-identity of the Gospel today? The christian theologians who insist on the need for doctrinal re-formulation are as concerned about "conserving" the truth once for all revealed, as are the more traditionally-minded theologians who stress doctrinal immutability. The progressive theologians regard themselves as the true conservatives: they are convinced that divine truth can be conserved only if it is proclaimed in a new way.

Biblical Hermeneutics

The hermeneutical question is not new in the Church. In the past theologians mainly dealt with biblical hermeneutics examining the principles necessary for the correct interpretation of the bible. How does one determine the meaning of biblical passages? The Catholic Church has always insisted, against any kind of biblicism or literalism, that to grasp the salvational truth of the scriptures, more is required than the study of the ancient texts: the understanding of scripture is influenced by the experience of the Church or, as we usually say, her divine tradition.

The ordinary Catholic treatment of biblical hermeneutics is usually divided into two sections.[9] The bible, we are told, is both a human and a divine book. To interpret the meaning of scripture, therefore, we need two sets of hermeneutic prin-

[9] See A. Card. Bea, art. "Biblische Hermeneutik", *Lex. f. Theol. u. Kirche*, vol. 2.

ciples, the first set dealing with scripture as a body of literature composed by men and the other dealing with it as a book of divine authorship.

The first set of principles spells out rules of literary criticism. Scholars must reconstruct the original text through textual criticism; they must study the language of the original work and engage in comparative literature; they must study the life of the author, his education, his character and his special concerns; they must examine the historical situation in which the piece of literature was composed and the issues with which it intended to deal; they must find the purpose for which the text was composed and the literary form to which it belongs; they must finally examine the history of formation of the text, i.e., the contribution of various traditions and authors on it. The first set of hermeneutical principles applies to the interpretation of any piece of literature. In the use of these principles the christian scholar joins the secular scholar in the interpretation of the scriptures.

Until recently the christian Churches have often hesitated to regard the bible as a human book and hence to apply the methods of literary criticism in interpreting scriptural texts. After one-half century of conflict in the Catholic Church, Vatican II has finally acknowledged the critical approach to the study of scripture. That the bible is the Word of God does not diminish its human character and, hence, does not dispense the christian scholar from using the scientific method for seeking a correct understanding of the text.

Yet, according to christian faith, the bible is the Word of God. This leads to the second set of hermeneutical principles which must be used by the christian interpreter of scripture. How do Catholic treatments of biblical hermeneutics usually set forth these principles?

The first principle enuntiates the inspiration of the scriptures and hence, their inerrancy. (Modern authors often point out, with Vatican II, that inspiration makes the scriptures an unfailing witness to God's self-revelation and that the inerrancy of scripture, therefore, refers to the salvational truth contained in it—not necessarily to the biographical, geographical, or historical information supplied in it.)

The second principle enuntiates the unity of the scriptures. Since the same God communicates himself through the entire scriptures, it is possible to interpret earlier parts of scripture in the light of the later parts.

The third principle asserts the Spirit-created unity between scripture and its understanding in the Church. The full meaning of a biblical text may be available only through the experience of the Church and the verdict of the ecclesiastical magisterium. In this sense, the magisterium is the guardian of scripture. Situations arise in the Church where the full meaning of the scriptural text is decided by the teaching authority.

The fourth principle affirms the unity of the christian faith. Christian faith is one because in it God communicates himself to man. For this reason scripture must be interpreted according to the analogy of faith, i.e., in harmony with the faith of the Church. This may mean that the interpreter of the bible must move beyond the literal meaning of the text to a wider meaning, the *sensus plenior,* that emerges as the text is understood in the total context of the Church's faith and life.

These hermeneutical principles, based on the divine authorship of the bible, tend to make us a little uncomfortable. They sound arbitrary. They seem to suggest that we do not have to pay attention to the literal meaning of the text; we seem to be free to understand it in the light of later parts of the bible and even of the Church's post-biblical experience. Is this not the manipulation of truth? Is it not offensive authoritarianism to suggest that the ecclesiastical magisterium may decide the meaning of a scriptural passage? These principles, formulated as they are, make us a little uncomfortable because we recall that they have been used to promote obscurantism, to resist the certain results of scientific exegesis and to suppress christian scholars dedicated to biblical research.

These principles are, nonetheless, part and parcel of a Catholic hermeneutics. I wish to explain their meaning in terms of the theology of faith and revelation developed in these pages. I propose that these principles deal with the subject discussed in this chapter, namely, the need to re-interpret the message of salvation to preserve its self-identity in a new historical situation. These principles make the strong affirmation—in terms of a concept of truth we no longer hold—that the Catholic Church is necessary for the salvational understanding of the Gospel.

When we say that the bible is the Word of God, we profess that it gives a unique and normative witness to the on-going self-communication of God to men. Through the bible, God addressed us. The bible refers beyond itself to God's continuing self-disclosure. It mediates the Word of God to the Church. This is what Christians believe. To the secular reader, the bible is simply a body of literature recording the experiences of Israel and the apostolic community. For the Christian, the bible is more than that: it points beyond itself and mediates an on-going reality in history. For the Christian, scripture speaks not only of what happened *then,* but also of what happens *now.* It is Word of God for the present. It reveals to us what is going on in the lives of men—in our own life— today. The faith of the Church that scripture refers to an on-going reality in history demands hermeneutical principles which go beyond the recognized rules of literary criticism.

Because scripture gives witness to the on-going self-disclosure of God in history, it is in need of being repeatedly re-interpreted.

This rule applies in a general way to all documents that refer to an on-going historical reality. Their meaning cannot be expressed once and for all. They have no meaning as such. They refer to a reality beyond themselves, and if this reality changes or develops, then they must be re-interpreted. If they are not re-interpreted, i.e., if their old meaning is re-affirmed in a new situation, then they cease to refer to the same on-going reality and hence betray what they were meant to say.

A simple example is a legal document. Laws always refer beyond themselves to an on-going society. Their meaning is derived from this society. If this society develops, the laws are in need of being re-interpreted. To affirm them in their old meaning according to the letter, would be unfaithful to their meaning according to the spirit. In a high school, if I may give a trivial example, a rule is made that the boys cannot enter the teachers' lounge. The meaning of this rule is clear. But what happens when the high school becomes co-educational? The students are now made up of boys and girls. If the rule is now affirmed according to the letter, the girls could enter the teachers' lounge. But this would go against the spirit of the rule which was devised to keep the students out of the lounge of the faculty. To preserve the identity of the society, the rule must be re-interpreted according to its spirit and then re-formulated. It must be made to say that all students, boys and girls, must keep out of the faculty lounge. The self-identity of the society demands the re-interpretation and the re-formulation of the laws.

Another example of a document (or spoken testimony) that refers beyond itself to a continuing reality are the words of commitment pronounced between people involved in a deep relationship. Because this relationship grows and develops, the sentences by which the commitment is expressed are in need of being re-interpreted according to their spirit and then re-formulated. On the first day of his marriage a man tells his wife that he loves her. The phrases he uses refer beyond themselves to a continuing reality, namely, his commitment in this relationship. If, after ten years, the man tells his wife that he loves her, he will use different words. He re-formulates his pledge. If he simply repeated the same phrases he had used on the first day, his wife would be startled by the sense of unreality. The words that were powerful on the first day would sound quite inauthentic after ten years. So much has happened between husband and wife. To express the unchanged character of their relationship, the husband must formulate his commitment in terms that take account of the common history that unites them.

These are two examples of a general rule. When a text refers beyond itself to a continuing reality, it receives its meaning from this reality and must be repeatedly re-interpreted in the light of it. If the text is understood according to the letter, its meaning is falsified. It must always be understood according to the spirit. What is this spirit? It is precisely the relationship of the text to the on-going historical reality to which it refers.

We now apply this general rule to the very special case of the scriptures. Christians believe, we said, that the scriptures refer beyond themselves to God's continuing self-communication to his people. The bible is more than the written record of the experience of Israel and the apostolic Church; it is the privileged and normative witness to an on-going saving reality in history. When theologians speak of the inspiration and inerrancy of the bible, they express the christian belief that the bible refers beyond itself to the on-going saving reality in the present. The bible does more than record the past: it mediates salvation now, it gives access to the saving mystery in the present. There are many other testimonies to divine revelation in the Church, but the bible is the normative witness by which the others are discerned and evaluated.

Since the bible is a document that refers beyond itself to, and mediates, an on-going divine reality in history, it is in need of being repeatedly re-interpreted in the light of this reality. This explains why the later biblical authors were able to re-interpret the meaning of earlier texts. This explains, moreover, why the christian Church has interpreted and re-interpreted the biblical witness throughout her history. A text which points beyond itself to an on-going reality, we said, has no meaning as such. It must be understood not according to the letter, but according to the spirit. Scripture must, therefore, be interpreted in the light of the on-going self-communication of God, to which it refers. It must be understood in the light of God's self-identical Word addressed to the Church now. For this reason Catholics say that the Church is the authoritative interpreter of the scriptures. The Church is a hermeneutical principle.

Literary criticism may be able to establish what a biblical text meant when it was written; but in order to find its salvational meaning now, the Church is necessary.

Here is an example. In Mark's gospel these words are attributed to Jesus: "He who believes and is baptized will be saved; but he who does not believe will be condemned" (16, 16). What does this sentence mean? The apostolic Church, facing a hostile world, was sent out to proclaim Jesus as the messiah, the savior, the one mediator between God and man. Those who accepted the Gospel became members of God's people; and those who rejected the preaching entered more deeply into the blindness and self-reliance that held them captive. To reject the Gospel meant to exclude oneself from life. The meaning of the Marcian text was that outside the Church there is no salvation.

But the scriptural witness refers beyond itself to the continuing self-communication of God. Later generations in the Church began to read the same Marcian text in a new light. They related it to other scriptural texts dealing with God's gift of himself. They were willing to understand the quotation in the light of the Spirit-created experience of the Church listening to the divine Word. Christians began to see in the text from Mark's gospel two distinct testimonies to divine self-revelation. First, the text testifies that God comes to men through the message and baptism of the Church. Secondly, the text testifies that God at certain times confronts men in such a way that they have only two choices: either they open themselves to him and live or they close themselves from him and die. The Marcian text gives witness to these two modes of divine self-communication. The apostolic Church tended to believe that these two modes always coincided. It tended to think that the moment of radical decision in a man's life is always present when the Gospel is preached to him. Over the centuries, listening to the self-identical Gospel in many new situations, the Church has learned to distinguish these two modes of divine self-communication. We believe that God comes to men through christian preaching and baptism and we believe that God confronts men with decisions between life and death, but we no longer hold that these two moments always coincide in the lives of men. The meaning of the text *now* is, therefore, different from the meaning *then*. The biblical text announces the Gospel today only if it is re-interpreted in the light of God's on-going self-communication in the Church. This re-interpretation has gradually taken place in the Catholic Church. At Vatican II in particular, the Church has declared, on the basis of a wider christology, that the divine summons which calls men to conversion is addressed to all men.

If a Catholic wished to understand the Marcian text according to the letter and insist that non-Christians are excluded from salvation, he would not follow the Church as the teacher of the Gospel. We recall that twenty years ago

Leonard Feeney was excommunicated from the Catholic
Church for teaching that strictly speaking there was no
salvation outside the Church. The tradition of the Church,
i.e., her continuing obedience to God's self-communication in
her, demands an on-going re-interpretation of past teaching.
We cannot be faithful to the Gospel of Christ by repeating
the letter of scripture and believing the message as enunci-
ated then; the Church, we hold, is necessary for the right
understanding of divine revelation.

Infallibility of the Church

Traditional Catholic hermeneutics, we have mentioned,
has always acknowledged the Church as a principle of interpretation. Usually this was applied only to the scriptures. We
have shown in the present chapter that this applies to the whole
of the Church's past teaching. Since the dogmatic teaching
of the Church's magisterium also refers beyond itself to the
on-going divine self-communication, it, too, is in need of
being periodically re-interpreted in the light of the Church's
Spirit-created experience. We cannot protect the Gospel of
Christ by repeating the biblical formulas or the ancient creeds
of the Church. A simple reiteration of these formulas today
does not communicate divine revelation, except perhaps to a
few people who have specialized in the ancient idiom. To
promote the Gospel—once for all delivered to the apostles—
in a new age, the Church must re-interpret it in the light of
God's present Word to her. The self-identity of the Gospel
is not protected by the immutability of doctrine: on the contrary, for the sake of conserving the Good News, the Church
must re-formulate her teaching.

These reflections enable us to assign a more definite meaning to the infallibility of the Church. Because of the many

changes that have occurred in the Church's official teaching and—let us be frank—because of the mistakes made by the ecclesiastical magisterium, the question has been raised whether it is still possible to speak of the infallibility of the Church and her ecclesiastical ministry. At one time, for instance, all the faithful including the magisterium understood the scriptures in a literal sense; thus, they supposed that the words attributed to Jesus in the gospels were actually uttered by him. Today the approach to scripture has changed. We are willing to use the methods of literary criticism; thus, we no longer claim that all the words attributed to Jesus were actually said by him. If the Church, people and ministry, can change their mind on such an important issue, does it still make sense to speak of infallibility?

A Catholic bishop has recently published a book in which he re-examines the question of infallibility.[10] Bishop Simons thinks that the New Testament by itself, read as a purely literary source, not only gives sufficient evidence for the central christian teaching on Trinity and incarnation but also affirms the role of the apostolic hierarchy and the primacy assigned by Christ to Peter and his successors. The New Testament, the bishop thinks, is the adequate basis for the certitude of the Church's preaching. There is no reason, he argues, to invoke the infallibility of the Church. The scriptures acknowledge the Church as the pillar of truth and the pope as the universal primate, but to interpret these gifts in terms of ecclesiastical and papal infallibility and of supreme papal jurisdiction over all Catholics, is going beyond the witness of the scriptures and engaging in pure speculation. Bishop Simons proposes that for the sake of a more effective proclamation of the Gospel in our day, the Church drop the

[10] Bishop F. Simons, *Infallibility and the Evidence*, Springfield, Ill., 1968.

claim to infallibility and understand papal primacy in terms other than supreme jurisdiction.

However much sympathy one might have for the practical suggestions of Bishop Simons, the theological basis for his argument is naive. The scriptures by themselves are not the adequate foundation of the Church's preaching. From the beginning of Christianity, the actual life of the Church has always been an hermeneutical principle for understanding the bible. It was only when the scriptures were read within the Church as the community of believers, open to the Spirit, that the doctrines of trinity and incarnation were understood as revealed in the scriptural witness. It was the experience of the Church, stirred by the Spirit and guided by the scriptures, that produced the historical evolution of the papal-episcopal system. For the sake of simplifying Catholic teaching and freeing the Church to change her mind on many issues, it does not help to suggest that Christians should be content with the scriptural witness alone. On the contrary, it is the Church's infallibility that enables her—or could enable her—to listen to God's Word addressed to her now and re-interpret the christian teaching as the Good News for the present age.

It is, of course, true that the term "infallibility" has usually been the symbol of the unchanging character of the christian teaching. In this chapter, however, we have seen that the Church listens to the on-going self-identical revelation of God and that, being equipped with an authoritative magisterium, she is able to shift the focus of the Gospel and re-interpret her past teaching in the light of the new focus. Because the Church with her collegial magisterium is infallible, it is possible to arrive at a consensus on the central thrust and message of the Gospel in a given age, a consensus which is recognized as normative in the whole Church and hence becomes an acknowledged principle of re-formulating Catholic teaching of the past. Understood in this way, the term "infallibility" becomes the symbol of the mutability of doctrine. Without infallibility a Church remains tied to the past. Without infallibility a Church gets stuck in the 1st century or in some later period. The gift of infallibility means that the Church is able to remain faithful to the past and is yet free to re-formulate christian teaching as the Good News for the contemporary world.

In the modern age, this process of re-interpretation has begun on an official level at Vatican Council II. Thanks to the Church's infallibility, i.e., thanks to her openness to God's Word addressed to her in the present, it is possible for her to re-interpret the creed and the body of Catholic teaching and, conserving the self-identical Gospel, to express them in contemporary language as a message dealing with the great problems of people today.

Select Bibliography

Babin, Pierre, *Options,* Herder & Herder, New York, 1967.

Bars, Henri, *Faith, Hope, and Charity,* Hawthorn Books, New York, 1961.

Baum, Gregory, *The Credibility of the Church Today,* Herder & Herder, New York, 1968.

Bellet, Maurice, *Facing the Unbeliever,* Herder & Herder, New York, 1967.

Blondel, Maurice, *Letter on Apologetics and History and Dogma,* Harvill Press, London, 1964.

Bulst, Werner, *Revelation,* Sheed & Ward, New York, 1965.

Chadwick, Owen, *From Bossuet to Newman,* Cambridge Univ. Press, 1957.

Dewart, Leslie, *The Future of Belief,* Herder & Herder, New York, 1967.

Dirscherl, Denis, *Speaking of God,* Bruce, Milwaukee, 1967.

Dondeyne, Albert, *Faith and the World,* Duquesne Univ. Press, Pittsburgh, 1962.

Geiselmann, J. R., *The Meaning of Tradition,* Herder & Herder, New York, 1966.

Gibson, Arthur, *The Faith of the Atheist,* Harper & Row, New York, 1968.

Guardini, R., *The Life of Faith,* Newman Press, Westminster, Md., 1961.

Heaney, John (ed.), *Faith, Reason, and the Gospel,* Newman Press, New York, N. Y., 1961.

Heijke, S. J., *The Bible on Faith,* St. Norbert Abbey Press, De Pere, Wisc., 1966.

135

Hermann, Ingo, *The Experience of Faith,* Kenedy, New York, 1966.

Hick, John, *Faith and the Philosophers,* St. Martin's Press, New York, 1964.

Johann, Robert, *Building the Human,* Herder & Herder, New York, 1968.

Joly, Eugene, *What Is Faith?,* Hawthorn Books, New York, 1958.

Journet, Charles, *What Is Dogma?,* Hawthorn Books, New York, 1964.

Latourelle, René, *Theology of Revelation,* Mercier Press, Dublin, 1968.

Meagher, Robert, *Personalities and Powers,* Herder & Herder, New York, 1968.

Mouroux, Jean, *I Believe: The Personal Structure of Faith,* Sheed & Ward, New York, 1959.

Moran, Gabriel, *Theology of Revelation,* Herder & Herder, New York, 1966.

Murphy, John, *With the Eyes of Faith,* Bruce, Milwaukee, 1966.

Rahner, Karl, *Belief Today,* Sheed & Ward, New York, 1967.
————*The Christian of the Future,* Herder & Herder, New York, 1967.

Richmond, James, *Faith and Philosophy,* Hodder & Stoughton, London, 1966.

Rondet, Henri, *Do Dogmas Change?,* Hawthorn Books, New York, 1961.

Walgrave, J., *Newman the Theologian,* Sheed & Ward, New York, 1960.